National Capital Region Network 2006 Forest Vegetation Monitoring Report

Natural Resource Report NPS//NCRN/NRTR—2007/046

John Paul Schmit
Patrick Campbell
National Park Service
Center for Urban Ecology
4598 MacArthur Blvd. NW
Washington, DC 20007

June 2007

U.S. Department of the Interior
National Park Service
Natural Resource Program Center
Fort Collins, Colorado

The Natural Resource Publication series addresses natural resource topics that are of interest and applicability to a broad readership in the National Park Service and to others in the management of natural resources, including the scientific community, the public, and the NPS conservation and environmental constituencies. Manuscripts are peer-reviewed to ensure that the information is scientifically credible, technically accurate, appropriately written for the intended audience, and is designed and published in a professional manner.

The Natural Resources Technical Reports series is used to disseminate the peer-reviewed results of scientific studies in the physical, biological, and social sciences for both the advancement of science and the achievement of the National Park Service's mission. The reports provide contributors with a forum for displaying comprehensive data that are often deleted from journals because of page limitations. Current examples of such reports include the results of research that addresses natural resource management issues; natural resource inventory and monitoring activities; resource assessment reports; scientific literature reviews; and peer reviewed proceedings of technical workshops, conferences, or symposia.

Views and conclusions in this report are those of the authors and do not necessarily reflect policies of the National Park Service. Mention of trade names or commercial products does not constitute endorsement or recommendation for use by the National Park Service.

Printed copies of reports in these series may be produced in a limited quantity and they are only available as long as the supply lasts. This report is also available from the National Capital Region, I&M Network website (http://www.nature.nps.gov/im/units/ncrn/monitoring_veg.cfm) on the internet, or by sending a request to the address on the back cover.

Please cite this publication as:

Contents

Page

Figures.. vi

Tables vii

Appendixes xi

Introduction.. 1

Methods.. 3

    Plot Locations 3

    Plot Layout.. 4

Forest Communities in the National Capital Region 7

    Tree Density and Basal Area 7

    Sapling Density and Basal Area 8

    Tree Seedling Density.. 8

    Tree Species Diversity 9

    Shrub Density 13

    Shrub Seedling Density 13

    Shrub Species Diversity... 14

    Coarse Woody Debris.. 14

Forest Pests and Diseases in the National Capital Region.................................. 17

Exotic Plant Species in the National Capital Region... 19

    Exotic Tree Species 19

    Vines in Trees.. 19

    Exotic Shrubs... 22

    Exotic Herbaceous Plants 22

Contents (continued)

Antietam National Battlefield 25

    Forest Communities 25

    Forest Pests and Diseases 26

    Exotic Plant Species 26

Catoctin Mountain Park 27

    Forest Communities 28

    Forest Pests and Diseases 31

    Exotic Plant Species 31

Chesapeake and Ohio Canal National Historical Park 33

    Forest Communities 33

    Forest Pests and Diseases 39

    Exotic Plant Species 39

George Washington Memorial Parkway 43

    Forest Communities 43

    Forest Pests and Diseases. 46

    Exotic Plant Species 46

Harpers Ferry National Historical Park 49

    Forest Communities 49

    Forest Pests and Diseases 53

    Exotic Plant Species 53

Manassas National Battlefield Park 55

    Forest Communities 55

    Forest Pest and Diseases 58

    Exotic Plant Species 58

Contents (continued)

Monocacy National Battlefield 61

    Forest Communities 61

    Forest Pests and Diseases 62

    Exotic Plant Species 62

National Capital Parks East 63

    Forest Communities 63

    Forest Pests and Diseases 66

    Exotic Plant Species 66

Prince William Forest Park 69

    Forest Communities 69

    Forest Pests and Diseases 73

    Exotic Plant Species 73

Rock Creek Park 75

    Forest Communities 75

    Forest Pests and Diseases 78

    Exotic Plant Species 78

Wolf Trap National Park for the Performing Arts 81

    Forest Communities 81

    Forest Pests and Diseases 82

    Exotic Plant Species 82

Literature Cited 84

Figures

Page

Figure 1. Layout of forest monitoring plots 5

Figure 2. Relative importance of tree species 12

Figure 3. Locations considered for forest monitoring in Antietam 25

Figure 4. Locations considered for forest monitoring in Catoctin 27

Figure 5. Locations considered for forest monitoring along the C&O Canal 34

Figure 6. Locations considered for forest monitoring in George Washington Memorial Parkway 43

Figure 7. Locations considered for forest monitoring in Harpers Ferry 49

Figure 8. Locations considered for forest monitoring in Manassas 55

Figure 9. Locations considered for forest monitoring in Monocacy 61

Figure 10. Locations considered for monitoring in National Capital Parks East 63

Figure 11. Locations considered for forest monitoring in Prince William 69

Figure 12. Locations considered for forest monitoring in Rock Creek 75

Figure 13. Locations considered for forest monitoring in Wolf Trap 81

Tables

Page

Table 1. Location and number of forest monitoring plots 3

Table 2. Tree density, basal area (BA) and species richness by park 7

Table 3. Sapling density, basal area (BA) and species richness by park 8

Table 4. Tree seedling density and richness by park 9

Table 5. Tree species found on the forest monitoring plots 10

Table 6. Shrub density and species richness by park 13

Table 7. Shrub seedling density and species richness by park 14

Table 8. Shrub species found on forest monitoring plots 14

Table 9. Coarse woody debris by park... 15

Table 10. Presence of vines in trees by park 20

Table 11. Species of vines in trees 20

Table 12. Tree species affected by vines 21

Table 13. Frequency of exotic herbaceous plants by park 22

Table 14. Frequency of exotic herbaceous plants by park 23

Table 15. Tree species found on the forest monitoring plot in Antietam 26

Table 16. Density, basal area (BA) and species richness of trees, saplings and
seedlings in Catoctin 29

Table 17. Tree species found on the forest monitoring plots in Catoctin 30

Table 18. Density, basal area (BA) and richness of trees, saplings and seedlings
on the C&O Canal 35

Table 19. Tree species found on the forest monitoring plots C&O Canal 36

Table 20. Shrub density and species richness on the C&O Canal 38

List of Tables (continued)

Table 21. Shrub species found on the forest monitoring plots on the C&O Canal 38

Table 22. Presence of vines on the C&O Canal 39

Table 23. Species of vines in trees on the C&O Canal 40

Table 24. Presence of exotic herbaceous plants on the C&O Canal 41

Table 25. Cover of exotic plants on the C&O Canal 41

Table 26. Density, basal area (BA) and richness of trees, saplings and
seedlings in GWMP 44

Table 27. Tree species found on the forest monitoring plots in GWMP 45

Table 28. Shrub density and richness in GWMP 46

Table 29. Presence of vines in GWMP 46

Table 30. Species of vines in trees in GWMP 46

Table 31. Presence of exotic herbaceous plants in GWMP 47

Table 32. Cover of exotic plants in GWMP 47

Table 33. Density, basal area (BA) and richness of trees, saplings
and seedlings in Harpers Ferry 50

Table 34. Tree species found on the forest monitoring plots in Harpers Ferry 51

Table 35. Shrub density and richness in Harpers Ferry 52

Table 36. Presence of vines in Harpers Ferry 53

Table 37. Species of vines in trees in Harpers Ferry 53

Table 38. Presence of exotic herbaceous plants in Harpers Ferry 54

Table 39. Cover of exotic plants in Harpers Ferry 54

Table 40. Density, basal area (BA) and richness of trees, saplings
and seedlings in Manassas 56

Table 41. Tree species found on the forest monitoring plots in Manassas 57

List of Tables (continued)

Table 42. Shrub density and richness in Manassas 58

Table 43. Shrub species found of the forest monitoring plots in Manassas 58

Table 44. Frequency of exotic herbaceous plants in Manassas 59

Table 45. Cover of herbaceous exotic plants in Manassas 59

Table 46. Tree species found on the forest monitoring plot in Monocacy 62

Table 47. Cover of herbaceous exotic plants in Monocacy 62

Table 48. Density, basal area (BA) and richness of trees, saplings and
seedlings in NACE 64

Table 49. Tree species found on the forest monitoring plots in NACE 65

Table 50. Shrub density and richness in NACE. 66

Table 51. Shrub species found on the forest monitoring plots in NACE 66

Table 52. Presence of vines in NACE 67

Table 53. Species of vines in trees in NACE 67

Table 54. Frequency of exotic herbaceous plants in NACE 68

Table 55. Cover of herbaceous exotic plants in NACE 68

Table 56. Density, basal area (BA) and richness of trees, saplings and
seedlings in Prince William 70

Table 57. Tree species found on the forest monitoring plots in Prince William 71

Table 58. Shrub density and richness in Prince William 72

Table 59. Shrub species found on the forest monitoring plots in Prince William 72

Table 60. Species of vines in trees in Prince William 73

Table 61. Presence of exotic herbaceous plants in Prince William 74

Table 62. Cover of herbaceous exotic plants in Prince William 74

List of Tables (continued).

Table 63. Density, basal area (BA) and richness of trees, saplings and
seedlings in Rock Creek 76

Table 64. Tree species found on forest the monitoring plots in Rock Creek 77

Table 65. Shrub density and richness in Rock Creek 77

Table 66. Shrub species found on the forest monitoring plots in Rock Creek 78

Table 67. Species of vines in trees in Rock Creek 78

Table 68. Presence of exotic herbaceous plants in Rock Creek 78

Table 69. Cover of herbaceous exotic plants in Rock Creek 79

Table 70. Tree species found on the forest monitoring plot in Wolf Trap 82

Appendixes

Page

Appendix A. List of forest pests and diseases targeted for monitoring in 2006 85

Appendix B. Woody plants monitored as shrubs in 2006 87

Appendix C. List of herbaceous exotic plants monitored in 2006 89

Introduction

Forests are the predominant natural vegetation in the eleven parks which make up the National Capital Region Network (NCRN, Table 1). Although many of the parks protect cultural and historic resources and provide recreational opportunities, all eleven parks have significant forest resources. In some cases, such as battlefield parks, historic forests are a cultural and well as a natural resource in that they help park visitors understand the events that took place in the park.

In 2005, the Inventory and Monitoring program of the NCRN listed 21 priority "vital signs", which are indicators of the state of natural resources in the NCRN parks (National Park Service, 2005). Forest vegetation is one of these vital signs. The focus of this vital sign is to track changes in community composition, such as species composition, growth rates and mortality rates of forest plants.

Three additional vital signs cover potential threats to forest vegetation. Deer density was selected as high deer density can lead to over-browsing of forest plants. Results from deer monitoring are not covered in this report. Two other vital signs, invasive plant species and forest insect pests and diseases, are covered in this report. Invasive plant species can crowd out native vegetation and could lead to changes in community composition. Insect pests and diseases can reduce populations of individual plant species.

To address these vital signs, in 2006 the NCRN began a long term forest vegetation monitoring program. The monitoring program consists of taking measurement of forest vegetation on a series of randomly located plots (Schmit et al. 2006). The plots are modified versions of those used by the Forest Inventory Analysis program of the US Forest Service (Stolte et al. 2002).

This report summarizes the findings of the monitoring program at regional and park level for 2006. As this is the first year of the program only summary data is presented and all results should be considered preliminary. Although some results, such as the presence of invasive species, are inherently undesirable, no formal assessment of the state of the parks is made in this report. Starting with the 2007 report, the NCRN plans to evaluate the status of the forest communities in the parks. The second round of sampling of the plots will begin in 2010. At that time the NCRN will be able to begin to evaluate trends in forest communities.

All raw data is available in electronic form directly from the NCRN.

Methods

Plot Locations

Forest monitoring plots have been established throughout the eleven parks that make up the NCRN. Plot locations were selected using a randomized design known as "generalized random tessellation stratified" (GRTS; Stevens and Olsen 2004). A GRTS design gives the investigator a spatially balanced (not clumped) and random set of sampling sites. The output of a GRTS draw is an ordered list of potential plot locations. If some of the locations are not suitable they are eliminated and the next locations down the list are chosen instead without the loss of spatial balance or randomness. This is particularly useful in the National Capital Region where current vegetation maps are not available for all parks, and cultural, archeological or other concerns may preclude plot setup on otherwise suitable sites.

In order to choose locations for the forest plots, ArcMap 9.0 was used to place a 250m grid over the entire region. Every intersection of the grid was a potential monitoring location. The 250m spacing was chosen as the NCRN will monitor forest birds at these locations, and bird monitoring points should be 250m apart (Dawson 2006). A GRTS draw was performed on this list of potential locations using S-Draw. As a result of this methodology the number of plots in each park over the 4 year sampling cycle will be proportional to the forest area in each park. During 2005 and 2006 the potential sampling locations were visited and permits were obtained from the parks to monitor suitable sites. In order to find 100 forest plot locations, 203 locations were considered, of which 103 locations were rejected. Locations were rejected for a variety of reasons including: being found in managed grasslands, roads or other non-forest habitat; being located off of park-owned property, or due to slopes steeper than 30°. After permits were obtained, plots were established at these locations and later measured by the seasonal monitoring crew. At least one plot was monitored in every park in 2006 (Table 1), but this was purely coincidental and may not be true of the next three years

Table 1. Location and number of forest monitoring plots.

Park name	Park abbreviation	Plots monitored	Locations rejected
Antietam National Battlefield	ANTI	1	7
Catoctin Mountain Park	CATO	7	0
Chesapeake and Ohio Canal National Historical Park	CHOH	25[1]	41
George Washington Memorial Parkway	GWMP	4[1]	4
Harpers Ferry National Historical Park	HAFE	7	3
Manassas National Battlefield Park	MANA	6	17
Monocacy National Battlefield	MONO	1	4
National Capital Parks-East	NACE	10	15
Prince William Forest Park	PRWI	35	7
Rock Creek Park	ROCR	3	5
Wolf Trap National Park for the Performing Arts	WOTR	1	0

[1]Two plots located in the Great Falls area on the Maryland side of the Potomac Gorge are on land managed by CHOH but owned by GWMP. Results for these plots are reported under CHOH.

Plot Layout

Each forest monitoring location consists of a 15m radius circular plot with an area of 707 m^2 (Figure 1). All trees ≥10cm dbh (diameter at breast height, 1.37 m) are identified, measured at dbh, tagged and mapped in the plot. Trees are also marked at dbh with forestry paint so that future measurements will be made at the same location on the tree. Also recorded is the presence of vines on each tree, targeted insect pests and diseases (Appendix A), and other conditions that could increase tree mortality.

Within the main plot are three 3m radius circular microplots, with a combined area of 85m^2. All saplings (trees between 1 and 10 cm dbh) and shrubs are identified, measured and tagged on these microplots. Saplings are measured at dbh and shrubs are measured at the root crown. Shrubs are woody species that are generally multi-stemmed. In practice, the field crew is provided with a list of species which are to be measured as shrubs (Appendix B).

Three 15m long transects radiate out from the center to the edge of the plot, which are used for measuring coarse woody debris. All woody debris > 7.5 cm is measured and assigned a decay class.

Finally, 12 1m^2 quadrats (0.5 m x 2 m) are placed in the microplots and along the transects. Cover of select exotic and native herbaceous species (Appendix C), and seeding regeneration is measured in the quadrats.

Forest plot design and measurements are generally based on that of the US Forest Service Forest Inventory and Analysis Program (FIA), but many modifications have been made. In general, the total area of the plot is nearly the same as that of the FIA plots (Stolte et al., 2002), but the NCRN plots are more compact. The more compact design was adopted as it is better suited to monitoring very small forest patches, which are often found in NCR parks.

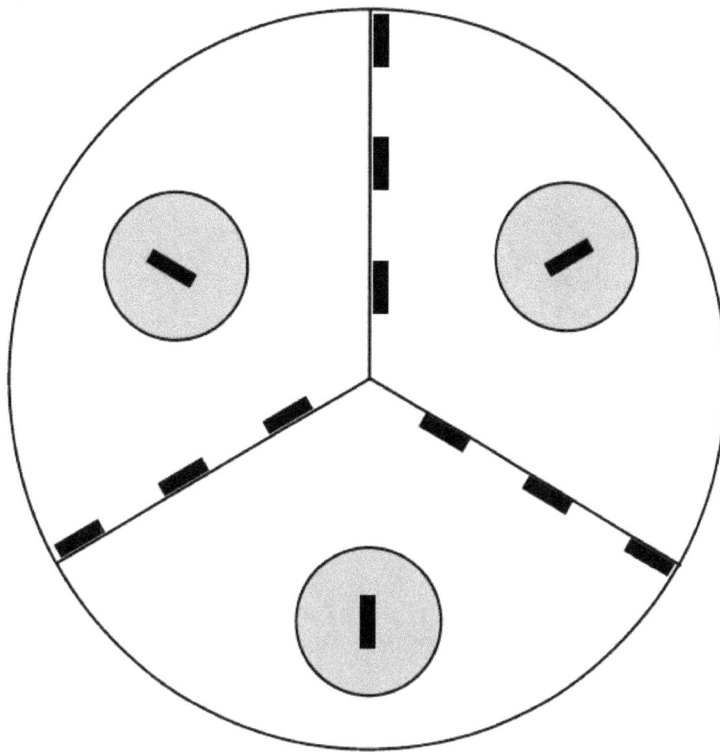

Figure 1. Layout of forest monitoring plots. Trees are monitored within the 15m radius white circle. Saplings and shrubs are monitored within the 3m radius grey circles. Seedlings and select exotic and native herbaceous plants are monitored in the 1m^2 black quadrats. Coarse woody debris is measured on the 15m long transects emanating from the center of the plot.

Forest Communities in the National Capital Region

During 2006, one of the goals of the NCRN was to gauge how many plots can be realistically monitored per year by our field crew. Before the field season began, a preliminary power analysis indicated that a minimum of 75 plots should be monitored per year, on a four year rotating panel for a total of 300 plots monitored every four years. However, additional plots would increase our ability to detect trends across the region and could substantially increase our ability to perform park-level analysis. Based on the field work in 2006, the NCRN program can monitor 100 plots per year. Therefore we have decided to monitor 400 plots on a 4-year rotating panel.

Tree Density and Basal Area

During 2006, a total of 2684 individual trees (dbh $\geq$10cm) were tagged and measured (Table 2). We estimate that once all 400 plots are installed, the NCRN will be monitoring over 10,500 individual trees.

Table 2. Tree density, basal area (BA) and species richness by park.

Park	Plots	Trees	Trees/ha	Total BA (cm^2)	BA/ha	Species	Species/Plot
ANTI	1	2	28	250	3,400	2	2.0
CATO	7	176	360	170,000	340,000	16	6.3
CHOH	25	615	350	440,000	250,000	36	6.0
GWMP	4	96	340	96,000	340,000	16	5.3
HAFE	7	156	320	110,000	220,000	28	8.0
MANA	6	206	490	94,000	220,000	20	7.3
MONO	1	38	540	15,000	210,000	5	5.0
NACE	10	241	340	160,000	230,000	25	7.2
PRWI	35	1052	430	650,000	260,000	27	7.7
ROCR	3	49	230	62,000	290,000	13	6.0
WOTR	1	53	750	28,000	390,000	7	7.0
Total	100	2684	380	1,800,000	260,000	55	6.8

The number of individual trees per plot varied from a high of 53 to a low of 0 in one plot. Plots with very low number of trees are typically located in areas that are in the process of succeeding into forest, but as of yet few trees have crossed the 10cm dbh threshold (e.g. the West Woods in Antietam). In general, plots found in the Piedmont (MANA, MONO, PRWI, WOTR and parts of other parks) have more trees than those found in other ecoregions (Ridge and Valley, Blue Ridge, Southeastern Plains). However, with only 100 plots installed so far, these differences are not statistically significant.

Tree basal area on individual plots varied from 0 to a high of 42,000 cm^2. Parks which have a high basal area/ha (CATO, GWMP) are not always the same as those with a high tree density (MANA, PRWI), although the lone plot located in WOTR is both very dense and has a high basal area. As with tree density, plots with low basal area are generally those in an early stage of forest succession.

In total, trees from 55 different tree species were found in the region, with most parks having considerably fewer. CHOH had the largest number of tree species, which is not surprising as many plots were located in the park and the park spans four different ecoregions. However, the highest average number of tree species per plot was found in HAFE. The number of tree species on individual plots varied from 0 to 13.

Sapling Density and Basal Area

During 2006, a total of 1082 saplings (trees between 1 and 10 cm dbh) were tagged and measured (Table 3). We estimate that once all 400 plots are installed, the NCRN will be monitoring over 4250 individual saplings. However, it should be noted that 243 saplings are box elder (*Acer negundo*) from a single plot near Noland's Ferry on the C&O canal, so this may be an overestimate.

In general, fewer saplings are monitored than trees. However, a smaller area is monitored for saplings (85 vs. 707m^2), so on a per hectare basis saplings are more dense than trees. The number of saplings on an individual plot varied from ten plots with zero to a single plot with 243. The plot with 243 saplings is clearly an outlier, as the next highest plot has 49. As would be expected, sapling basal area is much less than that of trees.

Table 3. Sapling density, basal area (BA) and species richness by park.

Park	Plots	Saplings	Saplings/ha	Total BA (cm^2)	BA/ ha	Species	Species/Plot
ANTI	1	3	350	76	9000	2	2.0
CATO	7	26	440	490	8300	11	1.7
CHOH	25	439	2100	5300	25,000	24	2.0
GWMP	4	28	830	500	15,000	7	2.0
HAFE	7	69	1200	880	15,000	12	2.3
MANA	6	58	1100	1000	20,000	14	4.0
MONO	1	4	470	200	24,000	2	2.0
NACE	10	69	810	730	8600	19	2.5
PRWI	35	354	1200	6000	20,000	18	3.7
ROCR	3	19	750	180	7200	4	1.7
WOTR	1	12	1400	320	37,000	4	4.0
Total	100	1082	1300	16,000	18,000	45	2.8

Only 45 sapling species were present on the plots as compared to 55 trees species Fewer individual saplings than trees were monitored, which likely accounts for some of this difference. The highest number of saplings species on a single plot was nine. As with trees, CHOH had the largest number of sapling species.

Tree Seedling Density

During 2006, 942 seedlings (trees less than 1cm dbh and >15cm height) were identified and their heights were measured (Table 4). We did not tag seedlings as this would be practically difficult and we expect them to have a high mortality rate.

Thirteen plots had no seedlings, and an additional seven plots had only one. On the other hand, four plots had over 40 seedlings, one of which had 53. There is considerable variation in seedling density across the region, even in relatively well sampled parks. Seedling density was notably low in Catoctin and Rock Creek parks.

A total of 39 tree species were found as seedlings on the plots, fewer than were found as trees or saplings. This is at least partially due to the fact that a smaller area was surveyed for seedlings and fewer individual tree seedlings were found than trees or saplings. The highest seedling species richness, 12 species, was found on a plot along the Baltimore-Washington Parkway in NACE.

Table 4. Tree seedling density and richness by park.

Park	Plots	Seedlings	Seedlings/ha	Species	Species/Plot
ANTI	1	7	5800	5	5.0
CATO	7	6	710	5	0.9
CHOH	25	218	7300	19	2.6
GWMP	4	40	8300	8	2.3
HAFE	7	47	5600	8	1.6
MANA	6	92	13,000	12	3.8
MONO	1	16	13,000	2	2.0
NACE	10	161	13,000	20	4.1
PRWI	35	336	8000	22	3.1
ROCR	3	6	1700	4	1.3
WOTR	1	14	12,000	3	3.0
Total	100	942	7900	39	3.9

Tree Species Diversity

Across the region, 59 species were found as trees, saplings and/or seedlings (Table 5). While a majority of these species were found in all three growth states, many species were found in only one or two. For example, American chestnut (*Castanea dentata*) was at one time a common, dominant canopy tree in eastern forests, but due to the Chestnut blight it is currently present only as a few seedlings and saplings. *Pinus virginiana* (Virginia pine) is the most common species in terms of individual trees. It is absent in the sapling layer, as it only establishes in early successional forests (U.S. Forest Service 1990), which were found on few plots. Pawpaw (*Asimina triloba*) is relatively rare as a large tree, but is the second most common species in both the sapling and seedling layer. Several local botanists have indicated to the NCRN that they believe this species is becoming more common, possibly because deer are browsing on competing species. A handful of species dominate the vegetation across the region (Figure 2) and this is more pronounced in the sapling and seedling layers than in the tree layer.

Table 5. Tree species found on the forest monitoring plots.

Latin Name	Common Name	Trees	Tree Basal Area cm^2	Saplings	Sapling BA cm^2	Seedlings
Acer negundo	box elder	204	73,000	295	3200	87
[1]*Acer platanoides*	Norway maple	1	170	1	1	-
Acer rubrum	red maple	193	65,000	41	790	26
Acer saccharinum	silver maple	49	113,000	2	69	13
Acer saccharum	sugar maple	18	9600	6	280	-
[1]*Ailanthus altissima*	tree of heaven	26	18,000	4	8	26
Amelanchier arborea	common serviceberry	1	140	-	-	-
Amelanchier canadensis	Canadian serviceberry	1	160	-	-	-
Amelanchier laevis	Allegheny serviceberry	2	180	3	79	6
Asimina triloba	pawpaw	8	880	146	1200	127
Betula lenta	sweet birch	18	6700	2	40	1
[1]*Broussonetia papyrifera*	paper mulberry	1	120	-	-	-
Carpinus caroliniana	American hornbeam	15	1500	17	340	7
Carya alba	mockernut hickory	105	42,000	17	330	22
Carya cordiformis	bitternut hickory	7	2400	1	2	7
Carya glabra	pignut hickory	84	48,000	7	160	13
Castanea dentata	American chestnut	-	-	3	12	4
Celtis occidentalis	common hackberry	35	17,000	-	-	23
Cercis canadensis	eastern redbud	2	160	2	100	2
Cornus florida	flowering dogwood	11	4700	32	750	3
Diospyros virginiana	common persimmon	2	340	16	36	6
Fagus grandifolia	American beech	207	74,000	141	2000	29
Fraxinus americana	white ash	34	19,000	9	180	38
Fraxinus pennsylvanica	green ash	24	18,000	7	120	63
Gleditsia triacanthos	honeylocust	-	-	-	-	1
Ilex opaca	American holly	25	3500	54	630	50
Juglans nigra	black walnut	24	27,000	1	13	-
Juniperus virginiana	eastern red cedar	118	28,000	27	860	1

Table 5. Trees found on the forest monitoring plots (continued).

Latin Name	Common Name	Trees	Tree Basal Area cm^2	Saplings	Sapling BA cm^2	Seedlings
Liquidambar styraciflua	sweetgum	55	26,000	12	120	58
Liriodendron tulipifera	tulip poplar	228	290,000	3	160	12
[1]*Maclura pomifera*	Osage orange	28	10,000	2	77	-
[1]*Malus baccata*	Siberian crabapple	-	-	1	17	-
Magnolia acuminata	cucumber tree	2	2700	-	-	-
[1]*Morus alba*	white mulberry	-	-	-	-	1
Morus rubra	red mulberry	2	320	1	17	-
Nyssa sylvatica	blackgum	150	42,000	87	2000	14
Ostrya virginiana	hophornbeam	3	820	-	-	1
Pinus taeda	loblolly pine	3	1800	-	-	-
Pinus virginiana	Virginia pine	279	200,000	-	-	4
Platanus occidentalis	American sycamore	32	55,000	2	85	-
Populus deltoides	eastern cottonwood	2	4800	-	-	-
[1]*Prunus avium*	sweet cherry	3	880	2	79	-
Prunus serotina	black cherry	37	29,000	6	89	28
Quercus alba	white oak	175	180,000	46	470	172
Quercus coccinea	scarlet oak	112	130,000	2	3	20
Quercus falcata	southern red oak	5	7100	4	100	1
Quercus palustris	pin oak	4	7000	-	-	-
Quercus phellos	willow oak	2	7300	-	-	-
Quercus prinus	chestnut oak	112	97,000	7	140	2
Quercus rubra	northern red oak	77	84,000	11	240	14
Quercus stellata	post oak	17	17,000	7	160	-
Quercus velutina	black oak	1	570	-	-	-
Robinia pseudoacacia	black locust	21	8200	-	-	1
Sassafras albidum	sassafras	5	890	12	350	35
Tilia americana	American basswood	7	7000	1	1	-
Tsuga canadensis	eastern hemlock	24	8700	11	95	-
Ulmus americana	American elm	1	1200	-	-	2
Ulmus rubra	slippery elm	79	32,000	14	330	10
Viburnum prunifolium	blackhaw	1	84	13	53	12

[1]Non-native species.

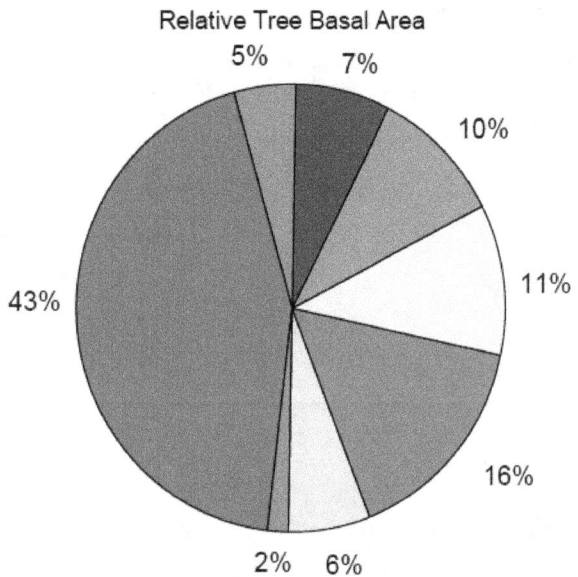

Relative Tree Basal Area

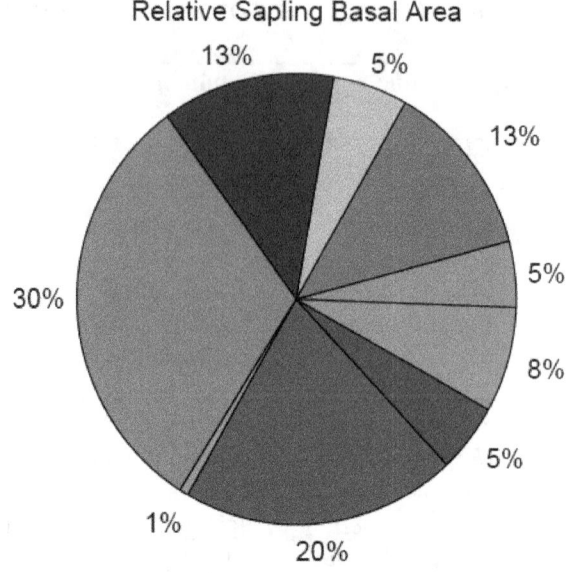

Relative Sapling Basal Area

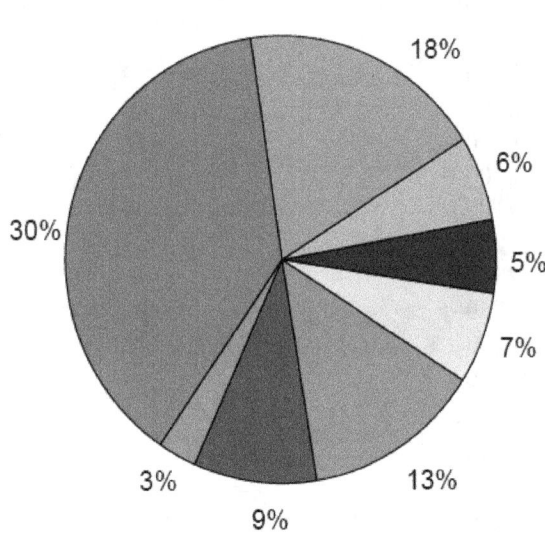

Relative Seedling Numbers

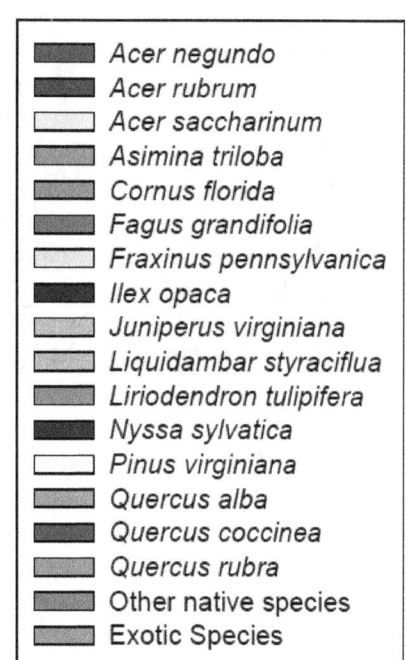

- *Acer negundo*
- *Acer rubrum*
- *Acer saccharinum*
- *Asimina triloba*
- *Cornus florida*
- *Fagus grandifolia*
- *Fraxinus pennsylvanica*
- *Ilex opaca*
- *Juniperus virginiana*
- *Liquidambar styraciflua*
- *Liriodendron tulipifera*
- *Nyssa sylvatica*
- *Pinus virginiana*
- *Quercus alba*
- *Quercus coccinea*
- *Quercus rubra*
- Other native species
- Exotic Species

Figure 2. Relative abundance and dominance of tree species. Pie charts show which species contribute over 5% to basal area or seedling numbers region-wide. No single tree species contributes over 5% in all three life history stages.

Shrub Density

During 2006, a total of 323 individuals from 13 shrub species (typically multi-stemmed with a diameter at root crown > 1cm [Appendix B]) were tagged and measured on the microplots in each plot (Table 9). We estimate that once all 400 plots are installed, the NCRN will be monitoring over 1250 shrubs. Some species that are commonly considered shrubs, such as multi-flora rose (*Rosa multiflora*) often grow as a dense cover rather than as individual plants. These species are monitored by measuring their cover on the quadrats, as it is impractical to tag and measure individuals. Shrubs are much less common than trees; 66 plots did not contain any shrubs. Several parks with few forest plots had no shrubs recorded.

Data on basal area of shrubs are not presented. During the course of the field season changes were made to the method used to measure basal area of shrubs. During the first half of the field season dbh was measured for shrubs. For the latter half of the field season, and for subsequent years, basal area of shrubs will be calculated using the diameter at root crown. As such it is not directly comparable to tree species; however, it is not useful to measure the dbh of a shrub as the dbh can be small even for a large plant. We will begin reporting basal area of shrubs beginning next year.

Shrub richness is considerably lower than that of trees. No plot contained more than three shrub species.

Table 6. Shrub density and species richness by park.

Park	Plots	Shrubs	Shrubs per Plot	Shrubs per ha	Species	Species per Plot
ANTI	1	0	0	0	0	0
CATO	7	0	0	0	0	0
CHOH	25	86	3	4100	4	0.5
GWMP	4	27	7	800	3	1.0
HAFE	7	83	12	1400	2	0.7
MANA	6	0	0	0	0	0
MONO	1	0	0	0	0	0
NACE	10	64	6	760	5	0.8
PRWI	35	61	2	200	0	0.4
ROCR	3	2	1	79	2	0.7
WOTR	1	0	0	0	0	0
Total	100	323	3	380	10	0.4

Shrub Seedling Density

A total of 389 shrub seedlings were found across all of the plots, far fewer than the number of tree seedlings found (Table 7). Only 31 plots had shrub seedlings present.

Shrub seedling density varied greatly across parks. GWMP and HAFE had much higher densities than the other parks, where as ANTI, CATO and MONO had no shrub seedlings at all.

Ten different shrubs were present as seedlings (Table 8). No park had more than three species present on the quadrats as shrub seedlings. Individual plots varied from zero to three species present as shrub seedlings.

Table 7. Shrub seedling density and species richness by park.

Park	Plots	Seedlings	Seedlings/ha	Species	Species/Plot
ANTI	1	0	-	-	-
CATO	7	0	-	-	-
CHOH	25	143	670	3	0.5
GWMP	4	57	1700	3	1.2
HAFE	7	75	1300	2	0.7
MANA	6	8	160	3	0.5
MONO	1	0	-	-	-
NACE	10	39	460	1	0.4
PRWI	35	51	170	1	0.2
ROCR	3	15	590	2	0.7
WOTR	1	1	120	1	1.0
Total	100	389	460	10	0.4

Shrub Species Diversity

Two shrub species, northern spicebush (*Lindera benzoin*) and mountain laurel (*Kalmia latifolia*) make up over 75% of individual shrubs (Table 8). These two species also accounted for over 79% of all shrub seedlings. The other native species are relatively rare across the region.

Table 8. Shrub species found on forest monitoring plots.

Latin Name	Common Name	Shrubs	Seedlings
[1]*Elaeagnus umbellata*	autumn olive	-	2
[1]*Euonymus alatus*	winged burning bush	1	2
Hamamelis virginiana	American witchhazel	4	1
Ilex verticillata	common winterberry	1	-
Kalmia latifolia	mountain laurel	68	57
[1]*Ligustrum obtusifolium*	border privet	10	32
Lindera benzoin	northern spicebush	178	251
[1]*Lonicera maackii*	amur honeysuckle	31	-
Staphylea trifolia	American bladdernut	25	29
Symphoricarpos orbiculatus	coralberry	-	1
Vaccinium corymbosum	highbush blueberry	4	-
Vaccinium stamineum	deerberry	-	1
Viburnum acerifolium	mapleleaf viburnum	-	13
Viburnum dentatum	southern arrow wood	1	-

[1]Non-native species.

Coarse Woody Debris

Coarse woody debris (CWD) was measured using the line-intersect method (Van Wagner, 1968) on three 15 m long transects in each plot. On average, there were 49 m^3 per ha of CWD across all plots (Table 9). The lack of CWD in Antietam is due to the fact that the lone plot monitored there is in the early stages of succession.

Table 9. Coarse woody debris by park.

Park Code	Plots	Coarse woody debris m^3/ha
ANTI	1	0
CATO	7	44
CHOH	25	43
GWMP	4	42
HAFE	7	48
MANA	6	16
MONO	1	45
NACE	10	66
PRWI	35	57
ROCR	3	77
WOTR	1	36
Total	100	49

Forest Pests and Diseases in the National Capital Region

Forest pests and diseases were selected as one of the 21 vital signs for the parks in NCRN. Forests in the parks have historically been impacted by pests such as the gypsy moth, and diseases such as the chestnut blight. Trees on the forest monitoring plot were monitored for a select group of pests and diseases (Appendix A). The list will be reviewed annually for appropriate additions or removals.

In 2006, relatively few trees were affected by forest pests or diseases. Three *Tsuga canadensis* in Catoctin were infected with hemlock woody adelgid. Gypsy moths were found in Catoctin on 31 trees of *Quercus prinus,* one of *Carya glabra*, one of *Betula lenta,* and one of *Acer rubrum.* Gypsy moths were also found on two *Quercus prinus* on the C&O Canal near the Pawpaw tunnel and a single *Nyssa sylvatica* tree on Maryland Heights in Harpers Ferry.

Exotic Plant Species in the National Capital Region

Many exotic plant species are found in the parks that make up the NCRN. Exotic plant species can exclude native species, may be less suitable for wildlife, and may have negative impacts on other aspects of the ecosystem such as soil quality.

The NCRN is measuring distribution and abundance of exotic plants species using the forest monitoring plots. Exotic trees, vines, shrubs and select herbaceous plants are monitored.

Exotic Tree Species

Of the 55 trees, five are not native to the region (Table 5). Tree of heaven (*Ailanthus altissima*) was represented by 26 individuals over nine plots, Norway maple (*Acer platanoides*) by a single tree in CHOH, paper mulberry (*Broussonetia papyrifera*) by a single tree in HAFE, Osage orange (*Maclura pomifera*) by 28 individuals on three plots and sweet cherry by three trees on three plots. Together these represent about 2.2% of all trees and 1.6% of all basal area.

As with trees, five sapling species are not native to the region. Norway maple was represented by a single sapling in ROCR, tree of heaven by four individuals at a single site in CHOH, sweet cherry by two individual at a single site in CHOH, Osage orange by two saplings at two sites in CHOH and Siberian crabapple (*Malus baccata*) by a single individual in NACE. Together these represent only 0.9% of all saplings and 1.1% of all sapling basal area.

Seedlings of two exotic species were found. Twenty-six tree of heaven seedlings and one white mulberry (*Morus alba*) seedling were found, which are 2.6% of all seedlings.

Based on the data collected in 2006, exotic tree species are present throughout the region but they represent a localized problem and are not currently a broad threat to forest communities.

Vines in Trees

The NCRN does not currently tag and monitor individual vines. However, vines are identified when they grow on tagged trees. Vines are noted and identified regardless of whether they are native, exotic, invasive, or non-invasive. Additionally, exotic vines which occur as cover on the quadrats are also monitored (see below).

In all, 393 trees, 15% of all marked trees, had vines growing on them (Table 10). Of these, 125 (4.7%) had vines growing in the crown of the tree. Vines that grow in the crowns of trees could increase tree mortality by shading leaves or toppling trees due to the increased weight. Vines in trees are particularly common in some parks, such as CHOH and NACE where forest edge is more common.

Table 10. Presence of vines in trees by park.

Park	Plots	Trees	Trees with Vines	Tree with vines in crown
ANTI	1	2	0	0
CATO	7	176	3	1
CHOH	25	615	163	59
GWMP	4	96	22	6
HAFE	7	156	32	14
MANA	6	206	1	0
MONO	1	38	6	3
NACE	10	241	104	33
PRWI	35	1052	52	5
ROCR	3	49	6	4
WOTR	1	53	4	0
Total	100	2684	393	125

Of the 12 species or genera of vines found, six were exotic species (Table 11). In total, 132 trees had exotic vines growing on them and of these, 52 had exotic vines growing in the crown of the tree. Native species, including *Parthenocissus quinque*folia (Virginia creeper) and *Vitis* spp. (wild grapes) were also very common.

Table 11. Species of vines in trees.

Latin Name	Common Name	Trees with Vines	Tree with vines in crown
[1]*Ampelopsis brevipedunculata*	porcelainberry	9	6
Campsis radicans	trumpet creeper	2	-
[1]*Celastrus orbiculatus*	oriental bittersweet	1	-
Convolvulus sp.	-	1	-
[1]*Euonymus fortunei*	creeping euonymus	3	2
[1]*Hedera helix*	English ivy	31	3
[1]*Lonicera spp.* (including *L. japonica*)	honeysuckle	66	30
Parthenocissus quinquefolia	Virginia creeper	111	24
[1]*Rosa multiflora*	multiflora rose	21	11
Smilax spp.	greenbriar	79	13
Toxicodendron radicans	poison ivy	77	32
Vitis spp.	Wild grape	109	54

[1]Non-native species.

Not all tree species were equally impacted by vines (Table 12). Over 10% of all individual trees of silver maple (*Acer saccharinum)*, pawpaw (*Asimina triloba)*, black walnut (*Juglans nigra)*, eastern red cedar (*Juniperus virginiana*), sweetgum (*Liquidambar styraciflua*), Osage orange

20

(*Maclura pomifera*), eastern cottonwood (*Populus deltoides*), black cherry (*Prunus serotina*), pin oak (*Quercus palustris*), American basswood (*Tilia americana)*, and slippery elm (*Ulmus rubra*), have vines in their crowns. In comparison, across all species, exotic vines are found in only 4.7% of trees. In some cases only a few individuals of a particular tree species were encountered and one of these had a vine in its crown, but for most species this is not the case. In future years the NCRN will determine if the same tree species tend to have vines in their crowns and if these vines have an impact on tree mortality.

Table 12. Tree species affected by vines.

Tree Species	Trees	Trees with Vines	Trees with Vines in Crown
Acer negundo	204	27	7
Acer rubrum	193	29	8
Acer saccharinum	49	15	11
Acer saccharum	18	2	-
Ailanthus altissima	26	14	-
Asimina triloba	8	2	1
Broussonetia papyrifera	1	1	-
Carya alba	105	5	1
Carya glabra	84	10	8
Celtis occidentalis	35	13	2
Fagus grandifolia	207	20	5
Fraxinus americana	34	10	2
Ilex opaca	25	1	-
Juglans nigra	24	12	5
Juniperus virginiana	118	36	23
Liquidambar styraciflua	55	22	7
Liriodendron tulipifera	228	21	3
Maclura pomifera	28	16	7
Nyssa sylvatica	150	17	8
Ostrya virginiana	3	1	-
Pinus virginiana	279	23	1
Platanus occidentalis	32	12	3
Populus deltoides	2	1	1
Prunus serotina	37	14	4
Quercus alba	175	7	-
Quercus coccinea	112	3	3
Quercus palustris	4	1	1
Quercus phellos	2	1	-
Quercus prinus	112	5	3
Quercus rubra	77	7	1
Robinia pseudoacacia	21	6	1
Tilia americana	7	5	1
Ulmus americana	1	1	-
Ulmus rubra	79	30	8

Exotic Shrubs

Of the fourteen shrub species found (Table 8), three of them are exotic and potentially invasive species. Winged burning bush (*Euonymus alatus*) was represented by a single individual in Rock Creek, border privet (*Ligustrum obtusifolium*) was represented by 10 individuals at a single site along the C&O Canal and amur honeysuckle (*Lonicera maackii*) was represented by 31 individual at 2 sites, one along the C&O Canal and the other in the Anacostia region of NACE. Together these represent 13% of all individual shrubs, and over 8% of all shrub seedlings. However, they were only found at four sites across the region.

Exotic Herbaceous Plants

On each plot, 12 quadrats measuring 0.5×2m are surveyed for targeted exotic plants. These include herbaceous exotics as well as some vines and shrubs such as multi-flora rose (*Rosa multiflora*) which cannot practically be monitored by tagging individual plants. Of the 100 plots monitored in 2006, 57 had invasive species on at least 1 quadrat (Table 13). No park was free from such species. The percent of plots with herbaceous exotics varies considerably between parks. For most of the parks the low number of plots surveyed makes it premature to draw any conclusions. However, looking at the two most sampled parks, clearly CHOH has a much higher percentage of plots with herbaceous invasives than does PRWI (Fisher's Exact Test, p<0.001). There are numerous differences between the two parks (forest patch size, distance to roads, distance to rivers, deer density, soil types etc.) and presently it is premature to assign the differences in invasive species cover to any particular factor.

Table 13. Frequency of exotic herbaceous plants by park.

Park	Plots	Plots with exotic herbs	% of plots with exotic herbs	Quadrats with exotics per plot with exotics
ANTI	1	1	100%	2.0
CATO	7	2	29%	6.5
CHOH	25	23	92%	9.3
GWMP	4	2	50%	10.5
HAFE	7	7	100%	5.1
MANA	6	4	67%	5.8
MONO	1	1	100%	12.0
NACE	10	8	80%	7.1
PRWI	35	7	20%	2.3
ROCR	3	1	33%	12.0
WOTR	1	1	100%	1.0
Total	100	57	57%	7.2

Fourteen exotic plant species were detected on the quadrats (Table 14). While most of the species were not widespread, several are found on a large number of plots throughout the region. These include two species, Japanese honeysuckle (*Lonicera japonica*) and multi-flora rose, that have a shrub or vine-like growth and three species, garlic mustard (*Alliaria petiolata*), Indian strawberry (*Duchesnea indica*) and Japanese stiltgrass (*Microstegium vimineum*), that are understory herbs. Some species, such as Japanese barberry (*Berberis thunbergii*), English ivy

(*Hedera helix*) and Japanese stiltgrass can cover a large percentage of the quadrats and plots where they are found.

Table 14. Cover of exotic plants.

Latin name	Common name	Plots	Mean % cover on quadrats where present	Mean % cover on all quadrats
Alliaria petiolata	garlic mustard	27	7%	4%
Ampelopsis brevipedunculata	porcelainberry	2	6%	1%
Berberis thunbergii	Japanese barberry	2	46%	21%
Celastrus orbiculatus	Oriental bittersweet	1	2%	<1%
Clematis terniflora	sweet autumn	1	5%	<1%
Duchesnea indica	Indian strawberry	26	6%	2%
Euonymus fortunei	creeping euonymus	1	11%	8%
Glechoma hederacea	ground ivy	12	16%	5%
Hedera helix	English Ivy	5	24%	16%
Lonicera japonica	Japanese honeysuckle	24	5%	2%
Microstegium vimineum	Japanese stiltgrass	31	20%	7%
Polygonum perfoliatum	mile-a-minute	2	4%	<1%
Rosa multiflora	multiflora rose	17	4%	1%
Rubus phoenicolasius	wineberry	8	5%	<1%

Antietam National Battlefield

Only a single plot was monitored in Antietam in 2006 (Figure 3). The plot is located in the East Woods section of the park which is currently being reforested by the park's natural resource staff.

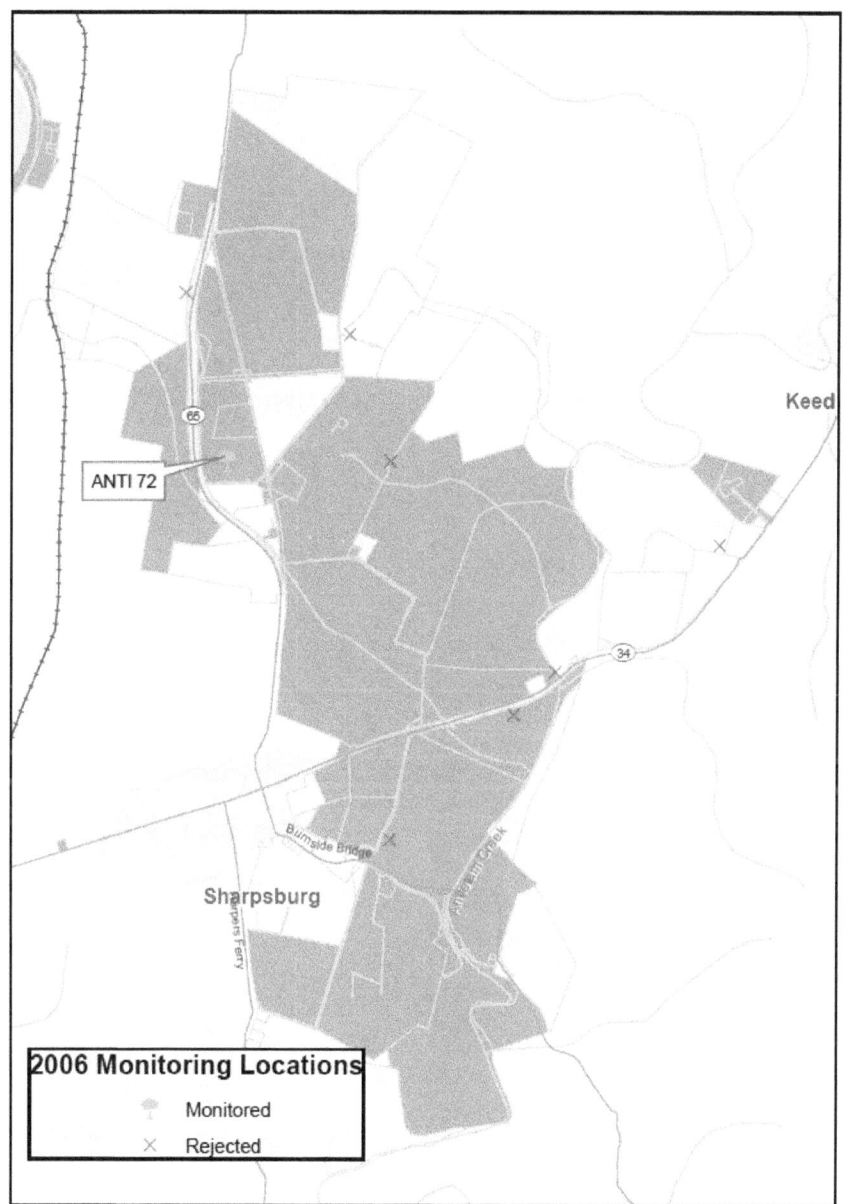

Figure 3. Locations considered for forest monitoring in Antietam.

Forest Communities

Density and basal area information for the single Antietam plot can be found in the tables above (Tables 2-4). In total, seven tree species were found in the forest plot (Table 15).

Table 15. Tree species found on the forest monitoring plot in Antietam.

Latin Name	Trees	Tree BA cm^2	Saplings	Sapling BA cm^2	Seedlings
Acer negundo	-	-	-	-	2
Celtis occidentalis	-	-	-	-	1
Platanus occidentalis	1	160	-	-	-
Juglans nigra	-	-	1	13	-
Prunus serotina	-	-	2	62	2
Quercus alba	1	85	-	-	1
Quercus rubra	-	-	-	-	1

No shrubs were found in the lone Antietam plot.

Forest Pests and Diseases
None of the targeted forest pests or diseases were found in Antietam.

Exotic Plant Species
The only exotic species found in the quadrats was *Rosa multiflora*. It was found in 2 quadrats. Based on cover data from the quadrats *Rosa multiflora* covered an average of 8% of the quadrats it was found on and slightly over 1% of the entire plot.

Catoctin Mountain Park

Seven plots were monitored in Catoctin in 2006 and no potential sites were rejected (Figure 4). All of the monitored sites were concentrated in the southeastern part of the park. This is an artifact from the random selection of the points rather than a plan to do different parts of the park in different years.

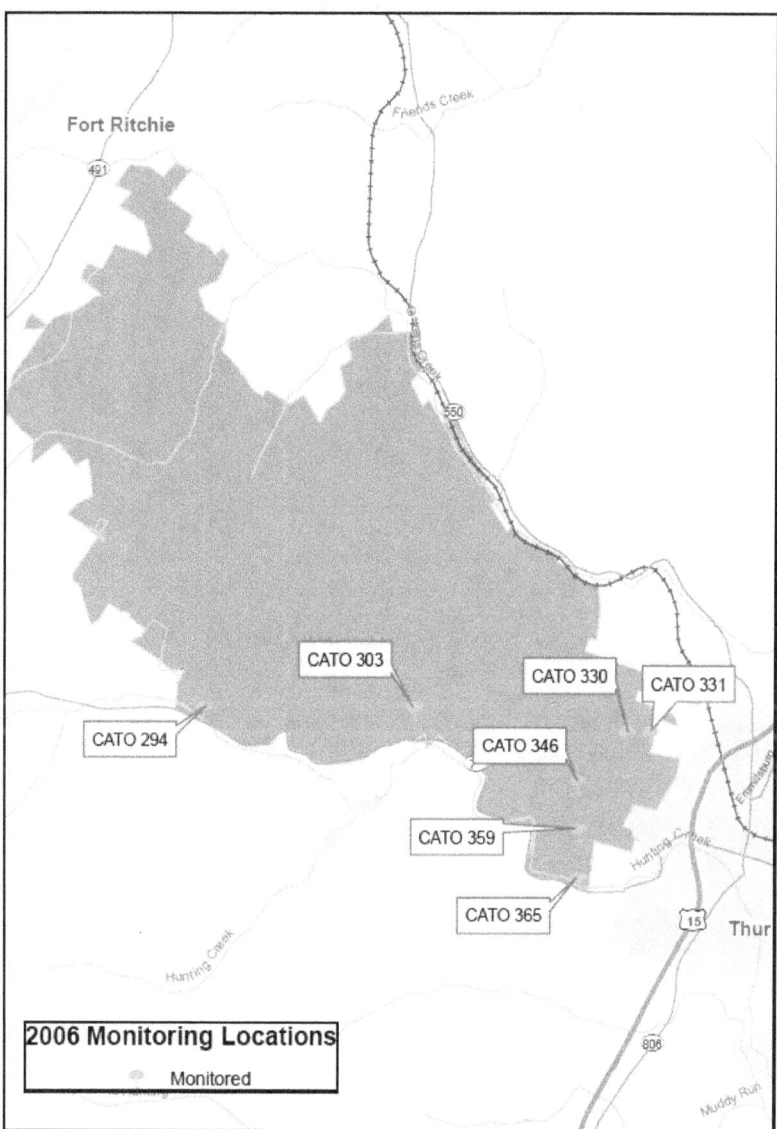

Figure 4. Locations considered for forest monitoring in Catoctin.

Forest Communities

There is considerable variation in tree density and basal area among plots in Catoctin (Table 15). The two plots closest to Big Hunting Creek, CATO-294 and CATO-365, have the highest number of trees per ha and the second and third largest basal area per ha.

There is also considerable disparity among plots in terms of sapling density, basal area and species richness. Nearly 70% of all individual saplings and over 40% of all sapling basal area were found in CATO-365 along Big Hunting Creek. All six species found as saplings in this plot were not found as saplings in the other six plots. Two plots had no saplings whatsoever.

Only six seedlings were found in Catoctin. Seedling density is less than one-tenth that of the region as a whole. On the quadrats of three plots, no seedlings were found.

Table 16. Density, basal area (BA) and species richness of trees, saplings and seedlings in Catoctin.

Plot	Trees	Trees/ha	Tree BA cm^2	Tree BA/ha	Tree Species	Saplings	Saplings /ha	Sapling BA cm^2	Sapling BA/ha	Sapling Species	Seedlings	Seedlings /ha	Seedling Species
CATO-294	39	552	31,000	430,000	8	1	120	61	7200	1	1	830	1
CATO-303	17	240	18,000	260,000	8	4	470	63	7400	2	-	-	-
CATO-330	22	311	19,000	270,000	4	2	240	114	13,000	2	-	-	-
CATO-331	22	311	22,000	310,000	4	-	-	-	-	-	-	-	-
CATO-346	23	325	38,000	530,000	5	-	-	-	-	-	1	830	1
CATO-359	19	269	18,000	250,000	7	1	120	50	5900	1	2	1700	2
CATO-365	34	481	22,000	320,000	9	18	2100	203	24,000	6	2	1700	2
Total	176	360	170,000	340,000	16	26	440	491	8300	11	6	710	5

29

In total, 19 tree species were found in Catoctin (Table 17). The only eastern hemlocks (*Tsuga canadensis*) found on the plots in 2006 were found in CATO-294 and CATO-365.

Table 17. Tree species found in Catoctin.

Latin Name	Common Name	Trees	Tree BA cm^2	Trees with vines/in crown	Saplings	Sapling BA cm^2	Seedlings
Acer rubrum	red maple	13	4100	-	2	27	-
Acer saccharum	sugar maple	2	2700	-	1	61	-
Amelanchier laevis	Allegheny serviceberry	2	180	-	1	17	-
Betula lenta	sweet birch	16	5000	-	2	40	1
Carpinus caroliniana	American hornbeam	-	-	-	2	46	-
Carya alba	mockernut hickory	2	290	-	-	-	-
Carya glabra	pignut hickory	19	8600	1/1	2	114	-
Fagus grandifolia	American beech	4	2600	-	2	17	-
Fraxinus americana	white ash	1	2000	-	-	-	-
Fraxinus pennsylvanica	green ash	4	3700	-	-	-	-
Liriodendron tulipifera	tulip poplar	19	30,000	1/-	-	-	1
Magnolia acuminata	cucumber tree	2	2700	-	-	-	-
Nyssa sylvatica	blackgum	7	3400	-	-	-	-
Quercus alba	white oak	5	7300	-	1	13	1
Quercus coccinea	scarlet oak	2	10,000	-	-	-	-
Quercus prinus	chestnut oak	43	50,000	-	1	50	1
Quercus rubra	northern red oak	10	26,000	-	-	-	-
Sassafras albidum	sassafras	5	890	-	-	-	2
Tsuga canadensis	eastern hemlock	24	8700	-	11	95	-

Only three native vines were found growing on trees in Catoctin. Virginia creeper (*Parthenocissus quinquefolia*) was found growing on two trees, a pignut hickory (*Carya glabra*) and a tulip poplar (*Liriodendron tulipifera*), but in neither case was a vine growing in the tree crown. Wild grape (*Vitis* spp.) was found once, growing in the crown of a pignut hickory.

No shrub species were found on the microplots in Catoctin.

Forest Pests and Diseases

Three eastern hemlock in Catoctin were infected with hemlock woody adelgid Two were on plot CATO-294 and one on plot CATO-365. Gypsy moths were found in Catoctin on 31 trees of chestnut oak (*Quercus prinus*) one of pignut hickory, one of sweet birch (*Betula lenta*) and one of red maple (*Acer rubrum*). These trees are located on plots CATO-330, CATO-331, CATO-346 and CATO-365.

Exotic Plant Species

No exotic trees, shrubs or vines were found in Catoctin. Only two exotic species were found on the quadrats. Japanese stiltgrass (*Microstegium vimin*eum) was found on all 12 quadrats in CATO-294, and covered 44% of the plot. Wineberry (*Rubus phoenicolasius*) was found on one quadrat in plot CATO-359. It covered 1% of that quadrat and less than 1% of the plot.

Chesapeake and Ohio Canal National Historical Park

Twenty five plots were monitored on the C&O Canal in 2006. The plots were located along the length of the canal (Figure 5).

Forest Communities

There is considerable variation in all measures relating to trees across the plots (Table 18). The group of low tree basal area plots near Nolands Ferry (plots CHOH-1045, CHOH-1055 and CHOH-1063) are forests in early stages of succession that are dominated by box elder (*Acer negundo*).

The C&O Canal has the highest number of saplings per plot and the second highest basal area per plot of any park in the network. However, the high number of saplings is due to box elder in CHOH-1045 and pawpaw (*Asimina triloba*) in CHOH-1342. These two plots, along with the box elder dominated plot CHOH-1055 also largely account for the high basal area of saplings. Nearly all of the remaining plots have below average sampling numbers and basal area.

Seeding density varied considerably across plots. Approximately 17% of all seedlings were pawpaw located on plot GWMP-94.

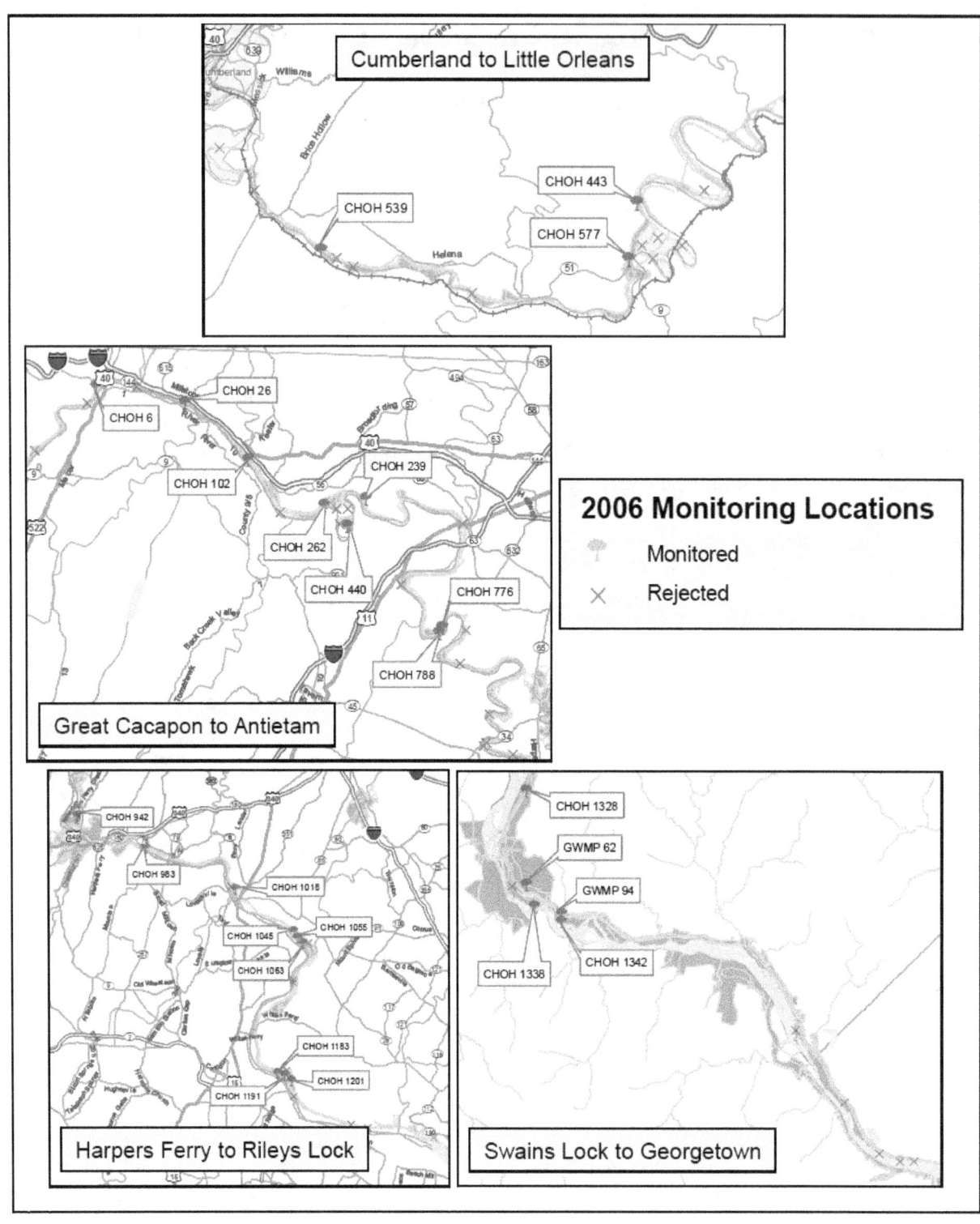

Figure 5. Locations considered for forest monitoring along the C&O Canal.

Table 18. Density, basal area (BA) and richness of trees, saplings and seedlings on the C&O Canal.

Plot	Trees	Trees/ha	Tree BA cm²	BA/ha	Tree Species	Saplings	Saplings/ha	Sapling BAcm²	BA/ha	Sapling Species	Seedlings	Seedlings/ha	Species
CHOH-6	21	297	11,000	160,000	7	-	-	-	-	-	5	4200	1
CHOH-26	11	156	33,000	460,000	2	-	-	-	-	-	4	3300	4
CHOH-102	17	240	17,000	230,000	3	3	350	57	6700	1	4	3300	2
CHOH-239	37	523	18,000	260,000	8	5	590	189	22,000	1	19	16,000	4
CHOH-262	25	354	23,000	330,000	6	5	590	24	2800	1	19	16,000	3
CHOH-440	19	269	21,000	300,000	5	1	120	19	2200	1	4	3300	2
CHOH-443	24	339	14,000	200,000	6	6	710	203	24,000	2	4	3300	3
CHOH-539	31	438	14,000	210,000	4	2	240	85	10,000	1	34	28,000	2
CHOH-577	33	467	12,000	170,000	8	10	1200	158	19,000	4	3	2500	2
CHOH-776	40	566	9400	130,000	4	13	1500	408	48,000	1	6	5000	2
CHOH-788	31	438	10,000	140,000	4	3	350	153	18,000	3	-	-	-
CHOH-942	35	495	27,000	380,000	13	6	710	185	22,000	5	2	1700	1
CHOH-983	14	198	31,000	430,000	3	5	590	138	16,000	2	-	-	-
CHOH-1018	26	368	21,000	300,000	9	14	1700	164	19,000	2	14	12,000	5
CHOH-1045	2	28	240	3400	2	243	29,000	1787	210,000	2	4	3300	3
CHOH-1055	46	651	6500	92,000	1	17	2000	447	532,000	2	11	9200	1
CHOH-1063	17	240	8700	120,000	6	13	1500	229	27,000	1	6	5000	4
CHOH-1183	20	283	33,000	460,000	6	2	240	62	7300	1	-	-	-
CHOH-1191	32	453	11,000	160,000	7	5	590	88	10,000	3	10	8300	7
CHOH-1201	22	311	13,000	180,000	6	-	-	-	-	-	4	3300	3
CHOH-1328	29	410	42,000	600,000	9	8	940	211	25,000	3	4	3300	1
CHOH-1338	27	382	16,000	230,000	9	6	710	72	8500	3	9	7500	6
CHOH-1342	14	198	11,000	160,000	8	42	5000	361	43,000	2	12	10,000	5
GWMP-62	24	339	15,000	220,000	10	7	820	103	12,000	3	-	-	-
GWMP-94	18	255	22,000	320,000	5	23	2700	132	16,000	5	40	33,000	3
Total	615	350	440,000	250,000	36	439	2100	5276	25,000	24	218	7300	19

Forty five different tree species are found on the C&O Canal (Table 19). One notable finding is that while silver maple (*Acer saccharinum*), tulip poplar (*Liriodendron tulipifera*), American sycamore (*Platanus occidentalis*) and northern red oak (*Quercus rubra*) are major components of the tree layer they are rare or absent as saplings or seedlings.

Table 19. Tree species found on the monitoring plots on the C&O Canal.

Latin Name	Common Name	Trees	Tree BA cm^2	Trees with vines/in crown	Saplings	Sapling BA cm^2	Seedlings
Acer negundo	box elder	123	37,000	8/1	286	2800	77
[1]*Acer platanoides*	Norway maple	1	170	-	-	-	-
Acer rubrum	red maple	25	7200	9/3	5	150	4
Acer saccharinum	silver maple	27	97,000	13/6	-	-	-
Acer saccharum	sugar maple	12	6600	2/-	5	220	-
[1]*Ailanthus altissima*	tree of heaven	17	14,000	8/-	4	8	9
Amelanchier arborea	common serviceberry	1	140	-	-	-	-
Amelanchier laevis	Allegheny serviceberry	-	-	-	1	17	2
Asimina triloba	pawpaw	7	790	2/1	78	580	65
Betula lenta	sweet birch	1	110	-	-	-	-
Carpinus caroliniana	American hornbeam	7	700	-	4	18	1
Carya alba	mockernut hickory	22	12,000	1/-	4	31	3
Carya cordiformis	bitternut hickory	-	-	-	-	-	3
Carya glabra	pignut hickory	14	6300	2/2	-	-	-
Celtis occidentalis	common hackberry	30	15,000	11/1	-	-	7
Cercis canadensis	eastern redbud	-	-	-	-	-	2
Cornus florida	flowering dogwood	-	-	-	3	65	-
Fagus grandifolia	American beech	9	7300	-	4	75	-
Fraxinus americana	white ash	19	12,000	5/1	2	87	15

Table 19. Tree species on the monitoring plots on the C&O Canal (continued).

Latin Name	Common Name	Trees	Tree BA cm^2	Trees with vines/in crown	Saplings	Sapling BA cm^2	Seedlings
Fraxinus pennsylvanica	green ash	2	1100	-	2	22	6
Gleditsia triacanthos	honeylocust	-	-	-	-	-	1
Ilex opaca	American holly	-	-	-	3	34	1
Juglans nigra	black walnut	17	12,000	10/3	-	-	-
Juniperus virginiana	eastern redcedar	43	11,000	31/21	14	470	-
Liquidambar styraciflua	sweetgum	55	26,000	-	-	-	-
Liriodendron tulipifera	tulip poplar	15	40,000	1/-	-	-	-
[1]*Maclura pomifera*	Osage orange	28	10,000	16/7	2	77	-
[1]*Malus baccata*	Siberian crabapple	-	-	-	1	17	-
Morus rubra	red mulberry	2	320	-/-	-	-	-
Nyssa sylvatica	blackgum	10	2500	1/-	4	51	-
Ostrya virginiana	hophornbeam	3	820	1/-	-	-	1
Pinus virginiana	Virginia pine	1	120	-	-	-	1
Platanus occidentalis	American sycamore	24	31,500	7/1	2	85	-
Populus deltoides	eastern cottonwood	2	4800	1/1	-	-	-
[1]*Prunus avium*	sweet cherry	2	390	-	2	79	-
Prunus serotina	black cherry	24	15,000	9/4	-	-	6
Quercus alba	white oak	9	8500	-	-	-	-
Quercus coccinea	scarlet oak	7	14,000	2/2	-	-	-
Quercus prinus	chestnut oak	35	22,000	1/-	5	64	-
Quercus rubra	northern red oak	24	34,000	-	1	4	-
Robinia pseudoacacia	black locust	13	5600	5/1	-	-	1
Sassafras albidum	sassafras	2	350	-	2	35	8
Tilia americana	American basswood	1	420	-	-	-	-
Ulmus rubra	slippery elm	35	11,000	18/4	4	110	7
Viburnum prunifolium	blackhaw	-	-	-	1	9	-

[1]Non-native species.

Shrubs were found at scattered locations along the canal (Table 20). By far the most shrubs were found on plots CHOH-6 and CHOH-26 in the Four Locks area.

Table 20. Shrub density and species richness on the monitoring plots on the C&O Canal.

Plot	Shrubs	Shrubs per ha	Species
CHOH-6	22	2600	2
CHOH-26	32	3800	1
CHOH-102	1	120	1
CHOH-239	-	-	-
CHOH-262	4	470	2
CHOH-440	7	820	1
CHOH-443	-	-	-
CHOH-539	-	-	-
CHOH-577	-	-	-
CHOH-776	-	-	-
CHOH-788	-	-	-
CHOH-942	-	-	-
CHOH-983	10	1200	1
CHOH-1018	4	470	1
CHOH-1045	-	-	-
CHOH-1055	-	-	-
CHOH-1063	-	-	-
CHOH-1183	-	-	-
CHOH-1191	1	120	1
CHOH-1201	1	120	1
CHOH-1328	-	-	-
CHOH-1338	4	470	1
CHOH-1342	-	-	-
GWMP-62	-	-	-
GWMP-94	-	-	-
Total	86	410	4

Northern spicebush (*Lindera benzoin*) is the most commonly found shrub on the C&O Canal (Table 21). Two invasive species, border privet (*Ligustrum obtusifolium*) and amur honeysuckle (*Lonicera maackii*) were also found.

Table 21. Shrub species found on the forest monitoring plots on the C&O Canal.

Latin Name	Common Name	Shrubs	Seedlings
Hamamelis virginiana	American witch hazel	4	1
[1]*Ligustrum obtusifolium*	border privet	10	32
Lindera benzoin	northern spicebush	71	110
[1]*Lonicera maackii*	amur honeysuckle	1	-

[1]Non-native species.

Forest Pests and Diseases

Gypsy moths were found twice on the canal, both times on *Quercus prinus* in plot CHOH-577, near the Paw Paw tunnel.

Exotic Plant Species
Exotic Trees

Five exotic tree species are found on the canal (Table 19). They make up 7.8% of all individuals and 5.6% of all basal area in the tree layer, 2.16% of individuals and 3.4% of basal area in the sapling layer, and 4.1% of all seedlings.

Vines in Trees

Vines in trees are common along the C&O Canal (Table 22). Vines were especially common on plot CHOH-776, near the midpoint of the canal, and on plots CHOH-1191 and CHOH-1201 near Edward's Ferry. On the other hand, no vines were found on trees between Swains lock and Georgetown. Most vines growing in trees on the Canal are native species (Table 23). However, two invasive exotics, honey suckle (*Lonicera spp.*) and multi-flora rose (*Rosa multiflora*) are common as well. Over 15% of silver maple (*Acer saccharinum*), black walnut (*Juglans nigra*), eastern redcedar (*Juniperus virginiana*), Osage orange (*Maclura pomifera*), black cherry (*Prunus serotina*) and white oak (*Quercus serotina*) trees have vines growing in their crowns (Table 19).

Table 22. Presence of vines on the C&O Canal.

Plot	Trees	Trees with Vines	Trees with Vines in Crown
CHOH-6	21	10	-
CHOH-26	11	2	1
CHOH-102	17	5	1
CHOH-239	37	9	2
CHOH-262	25	12	1
CHOH-440	19	6	2
CHOH-443	24	7	2
CHOH-539	31	2	0
CHOH-577	33	-	-
CHOH-776	40	29	21
CHOH-788	31	11	3
CHOH-942	35	8	6
CHOH-983	14	4	2
CHOH-1018	26	7	2
CHOH-1045	2	-	-
CHOH-1055	46	2	1
CHOH-1063	17	4	3
CHOH-1183	20	3	2
CHOH-1191	32	24	7
CHOH-1201	22	18	3
CHOH-1328	29	-	-
CHOH-1338	27	-	-
CHOH-1342	14	-	-
GWMP-62	24	-	-
GWMP-94	18	-	-
Total	615	163	59

Table 23. Species of vines in trees on the C&O Canal.

Latin Name	Common Name	Trees with Vines	Tree with vines in crown
Campsis radicans	trumpet creeper	1	-
Convolvulus sp.	-	1	-
[1]*Euonymus fortunei*	creeping euonymus	3	2
[1]*Hedera helix*	English ivy	1	-
[1]*Lonicera spp.* (including *L. japonica*)	honeysuckle	33	18
Parthenocissus quinquefolia	Virginia creeper	68	17
[1]*Rosa multiflora*	multiflora rose	16	9
Smilax spp.	greenbriar	10	1
Toxicodendron radicans	poison ivy	24	9
Vitis spp.	Wild grape	67	31

[1] Non-native species.

Exotic Shrubs

Two invasive shrub species were found (Table 21). Ten individuals of Border privet (*Ligustrum obtusifolium*) were found on CHOH-6 near Hancock, and one amur honeysuckle (*Lonicera maackii*) was found on CHOH -262 near Four Locks.

Exotic Herbaceous Plants

Exotic herbaceous plants are very common on the C&O Canal. All but two plots, and over 70% of all quadrats monitored, had exotic plants growing on them. Nearly all plots have multiple exotic species.

Table 24. Presence of exotic herbaceous plants on the C&O Canal.

Plot	Quadrats with Exotics	Number of Exotic Species
CHOH-6	10	3
CHOH-26	11	1
CHOH-102	12	5
CHOH-239	12	6
CHOH-262	12	6
CHOH-440	12	7
CHOH-443	9	3
CHOH-539	12	5
CHOH-577	8	3
CHOH-776	9	6
CHOH-788	12	4
CHOH-942	7	1
CHOH-983	12	4
CHOH-1018	11	5
CHOH-1045	8	2
CHOH-1055	10	3
CHOH-1063	4	3
CHOH-1183	12	3
CHOH-1191	8	4
CHOH-1201	12	4
CHOH-1328	-	-
CHOH-1338	1	1
CHOH-1342	11	2
GWMP-62	-	-
GWMP-94	1	1
Total	216	10

Ten species of exotic herbaceous plants were found on the canal (Table 25).

Table 25. Cover of exotic plants on the C&O Canal.

Latin name	Common name	Plots	Mean % cover on quadrats where present	Mean % cover on all quadrats
Alliaria petiolata	garlic mustard	18	7%	4%
Berberis thunbergii	Japanese barberry	2	46%	21%
Celastrus orbiculatus	Oriental bittersweet	1	2%	<1%
Duchesnea indica	Indian strawberry	14	6%	2%
Euonymus fortunei	creeping euonymus	1	11%	8%
Glechoma hederacea	ground ivy	8	18%	6%
Lonicera japonica	Japanese honeysuckle	10	7%	4%
Microstegium vimineum	Japanese stiltgrass	15	21%	9%
Rosa multiflora	multiflora rose	11	5%	2%
Rubus phoenicolasius	wineberry	2	9%	1%

George Washington Memorial Parkway

Four plots were monitored along GWMP in 2006. Two plots are on Theodore Roosevelt Island, one is near Mount Vernon and the one is in Great Falls Park (Figure 6).

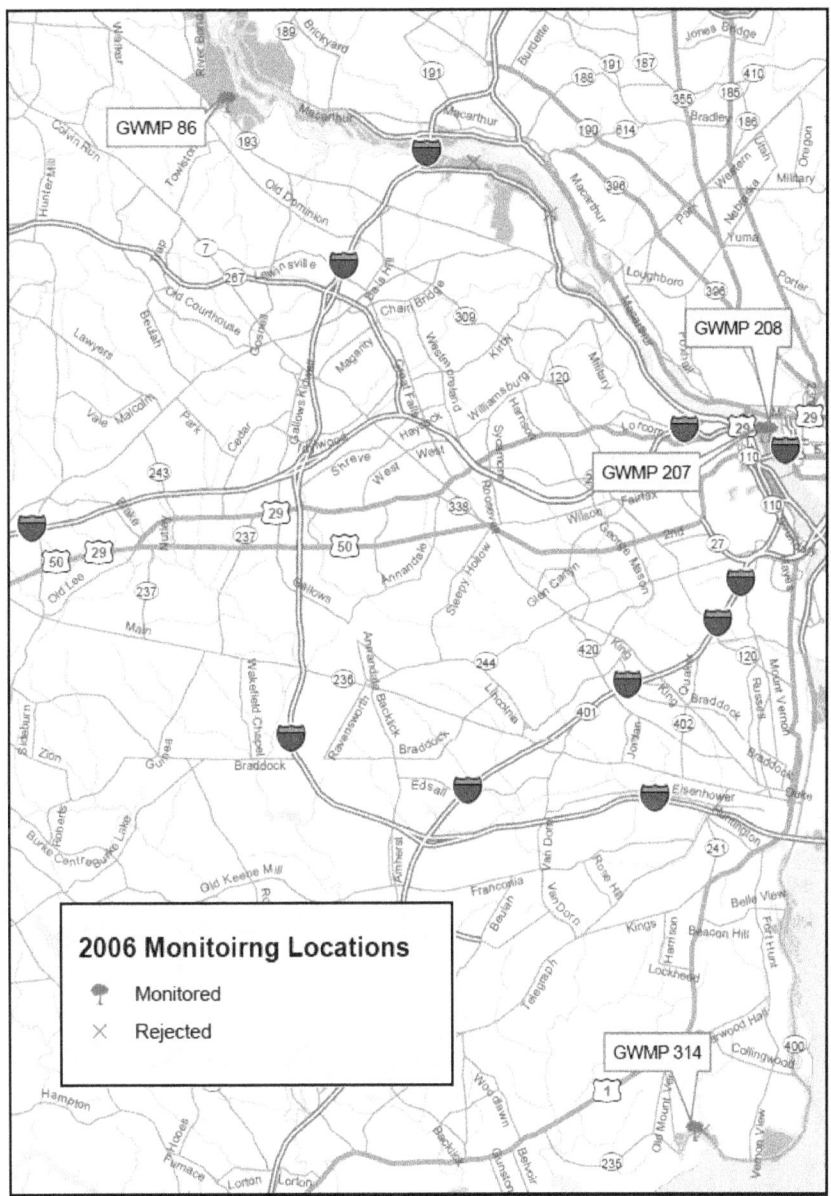

Figure 6. Locations considered for forest monitoring in George Washington Memorial Parkway

Forest Communities
Density and basal area information for the four plots is presented in Table 26. In total, 21 tree species were found in the four plots (Table 27).

Table 26. Density, basal area (BA) and richness of trees, saplings and seedlings in GWMP.

Plot	Trees	Trees/ha	Tree BA cm^2	BA/ha	Tree Species	Saplings	Saplings/ha	Sapling BA cm^2	BA/ha	Sapling Species	Seedlings	Seedlings/ha	Species
GWMP-86	22	310	14,000	200,000	5	18	2100	210	24,000	4	-	-	-
GWMP-207	17	240	32,000	450,000	4	2	240	70	8200	2	19	16,000	4
GWMP-208	29	410	25,000	360,000	4	-	-	-	-	-	21	18,000	5
GWMP-314	28	400	24,000	340,000	8	8	940	220	26,000	2	-	-	-
Total	96	340	96,000	340,000	17	28	830	500	15,000	7	40	8300	8

Table 27. Tree species found on the forest monitoring plots in GWMP.

Latin Name	Common Name	Trees	Tree BA cm^2	Trees with vines/in crown	Saplings	Sapling BA cm^2	Seedlings
Acer negundo	box elder	30	19,000	10/4	1	68	2
Acer rubrum	red maple	1	85	-	-	-	-
Acer saccharinum	silver maple	3	4700	2/2	-	-	13
[1]*Ailanthus altissima*	tree of heaven	4	1600	4/-	-	-	13
Amelanchier canadensis	Canadian serviceberry	1	160	-	-	-	-
Asimina triloba	pawpaw	8	880	-	-	-	-
Carya alba	mockernut hickory	1	160	-	2	85	-
Carya cordiformis	bitternut hickory	-	-	-	1	2	3
Fagus grandifolia	American beech	14	4300	-	8	150	-
Fraxinus americana	white ash	-	-	-	-	-	2
Fraxinus pennsylvanica	green ash	2	8300	-	-	-	5
Liquidambar styraciflua	sweetgum	1	360	-	-	-	-
Liriodendron tulipifera	tulip poplar	6	22,000	5/-	-	-	-
[1]*Morus alba*	white mulberry	-	-	-	-	-	1
Nyssa sylvatica	blackgum	2	1800	-	14	140	-
Quercus alba	white oak	6	8600	-	1	40	-
Quercus coccinea	scarlet oak	2	18,000	-	-	-	-
Quercus prinus	chestnut oak	4	1200	-	-	-	-
Quercus rubra	northern red oak	3	4900	1/-	-	-	-
Sassafras albidum	sassafras	5	890	-	1	10	-
Ulmus rubra	slippery elm	1	93	-	-	-	1

[1]Non-native species.

Shrubs were found in three of the four GWMP plots monitored in 2006 (Table 28). Only three shrub species were found, nine mountain laurel (*Kalmia latifolia*) shrubs and six seedlings, 11 spicebush (*Lindera benzoin*) shrubs and 31 seedlings, and seven American bladdernut (*Staphylea trifolia*) shrubs and 20 seedlings.

Table 28. Shrub density and richness in GWMP.

Plot	Shrubs	Shrubs per ha	Species
GWMP-86	9	1100	1
GWMP-207	10	1200	2
GWMP-208	8	940	1
GWMP-314	-	-	-
Total	27	800	3

Forest Pests and Diseases.
No trees were infected by any of the target pest or disease species.

Exotic Plant Species
Exotic Trees
While there are only four trees and no saplings of exotic species, over 30% of all seedlings found were tree of heaven (*Ailanthus altissima* [Table 27]).

Vines in Trees
Vines in trees are common in the plots on Theodore Roosevelt Island (Table 29). The exotic vine English ivy (*Hedera helix*) was the most common species (Table 30).

Table 29. Presence of vines in GWMP.

Plot	Trees	Trees with Vines	Trees with Vines in Crown
GWMP-86	22	-	-
GWMP-207	21	16	-
GWMP-208	11	6	6
GWMP-314	28	-	-
Total	96	22	6

Table 30. Species of vines in trees in GWMP

Latin Name	Common Name	Trees with Vines	Tree with vines in crown
[1]*Celastrus orbiculatus*	oriental bittersweet	1	-
[1]*Hedera helix*	English ivy	15	1
Parthenocissus quinquefolia	Virginia creeper	1	-
Toxicodendron radicans	poison ivy	6	6
Vitis spp.	Wild grape	3	-

[1] Non-native species.

Exotic Shrubs
No non-native shrubs were found.

Exotic Herbaceous Species

Exotic herbaceous plants are common on the two plots on Theodore Roosevelt Island (Table 31). Ground ivy (*Glechoma hederacea*) and English ivy are the most common species (Table 32).

Table 31. Presence of exotic herbaceous plants in GWMP.

Plot	Quadrats with Exotics	Number of Exotic Species
GWMP-86	-	-
GWMP-207	12	4
GWMP-208	9	4
GWMP-314	-	-
Total	21	6

Table 32. Cover of exotic plants in GWMP.

Latin name	Common name	Plots	Mean % cover on quadrats where present	Mean % cover on all quadrats
Alliaria petiolata	garlic mustard	2	3%	1%
Duchesnea indica	Indian strawberry	1	1%	<1%
Glechoma hederacea	ground ivy	2	18%	4%
Hedera helix	English ivy	2	20%	15%
Lonicera japonica	Japanese honeysuckle	1	1%	<1%
Microstegium vimineum	Japanese stiltgrass	1	1%	<1%

Harpers Ferry National Historical Park

Seven plots were monitored in Harper's Ferry in 2006 (Figure 7).

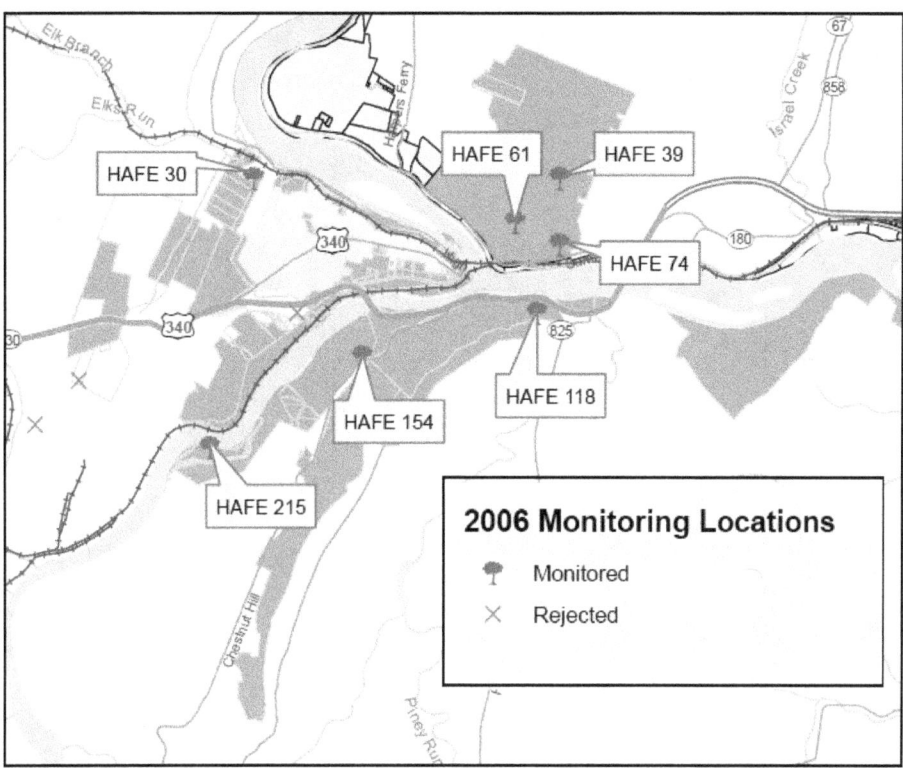

Figure 7. Locations considered for forest monitoring in Harpers Ferry.

Forest Communities

In general, plots in Harpers Ferry have a moderate density and basal area compared to other parks, but they are quite diverse (Table 33). Plots in the Maryland Heights section of the park (HAFE-39, HAFE-61 and HAFE-74) have fewer seedlings than the rest of the park, and two of these plots have no saplings.

Thirty nine different tree species are found on the plots in Harpers Ferry (Table 34). Much of the regeneration that is taking place in the park is pawpaw (*Asimina triloba*).

Table 33. Density, basal area (BA) and richness of trees, saplings and seedlings in Harpers Ferry.

Plot	Trees	Trees/ha	Tree BA cm²	BA/ha	Tree Species	Saplings	Saplings/ha	Sapling BA cm²	Sapling BA/ha	Sapling Species	Seedlings	Seedlings/ha	Species
HAFE-30	18	250	15,000	210,000	9	2	230	57	6700	2	13	11,000	3
HAFE-39	28	400	17,000	240,000	9	7	820	200	24,000	5	-	-	-
HAFE-61	30	420	10,000	150,000	7	-	-	-	-	-	1	830	1
HAFE-74	24	340	10,000	140,000	8	-	-	-	-	-	1	830	1
HAFE-118	16	230	15,000	220,000	12	49	5800	510	60,000	4	16	13,000	1
HAFE-154	19	270	17,000	250,000	4	5	590	88	10,000	3	11	9200	4
HAFE-215	21	300	25,000	350,000	7	6	710	14	1600	2	5	4200	1
Total	146	320	110,000	220,000	28	69	1200	870	15,000	12	47	5600	7

Table 34. Tree species found on the forest monitoring plots in Harpers Ferry.

Latin Name	Common Name	Trees	Tree BA cm^2	Trees with vines/in crown	Saplings	Sapling BA cm^2	Seedlings
Acer negundo	box elder	14	5700	3/-	2	57	-
Acer rubrum	red maple	16	7800	3/1	-	-	1
Acer saccharinum	silver maple	-	-	-	1	19	-
[1]*Ailanthus altissima*	tree of heaven	4	1200	1/-	-	-	1
Amelanchier laevis	Allegheny serviceberry	-	-	-	1	46	-
Asimina triloba	pawpaw	1	87	-	52	470	33
Betula lenta	sweet birch	1	1600	-	-	-	-
[1]*Broussonetia papyrifera*	paper mulberry	1	120	1/-	-	-	-
Carya alba	mockernut hickory	12	3300	3/1	2	10	-
Carya cordiformis	bitternut hickory	1	1300	-	1	2	1
Carya glabra	pignut hickory	18	8700	4/4	-	-	-
Celtis occidentalis	common hackberry	5	2500	2/1	-	-	1
Cercis canadensis	eastern redbud	1	82	-	2	100	-
Cornus florida	flowering dogwood	-	-	-	32	750	-
Diospyros virginiana	common persimmon	-	-	-	-	-	1
Fagus grandifolia	American beech	2	190	1/1	-	-	-
Fraxinus americana	white ash	8	3800	4/1	2	52	8
Fraxinus pennsylvanica	green ash	-	-	-	7	120	-
Ilex opaca	American holly	-	-	-	-	-	-
Juglans nigra	black walnut	3	11,000	2/2	-	-	-
Juniperus virginiana	eastern redcedar	-	-	-	-	-	-
Liquidambar styraciflua	sweetgum	-	-	-	-	-	-
Liriodendron tulipifera	tulip poplar	15	23,000	1/-	-	-	-
Nyssa sylvatica	blackgum	9	1900	1/-	1	8	-
Pinus virginiana	Virginia pine	1	330	-	-	-	-

Table 34. Tree species found on the forest monitoring plots in Harpers Ferry (continued).

Latin Name	Common Name	Trees	Tree BA cm^2	Trees with vines/in crown	Saplings	Sapling BA cm^2	Seedlings
Platanus occidentalis	American sycamore	2	8500	1/-	-	-	-
Populus deltoides	eastern cottonwood	-	-	-	-	-	-
[1]*Prunus avium*	sweet cherry	1	490	-	-	-	-
Prunus serotina	black cherry	1	1400	-	1	1	-
Quercus coccinea	scarlet oak	7	5900	1/1	-	-	-
Quercus falcata	southern red oak	5	7100	-	-	-	-
Quercus palustris	pin oak	1	2500	1/1	-	-	-
Quercus prinus	chestnut oak	18	13,000	1/1	-	-	1
Quercus rubra	northern red oak	4	740	-	-	-	-
Quercus stellata	post oak	1	390	1/-	-	-	-
Robinia pseudoacacia	black locust	1	150	-	-	-	-
Sassafras albidum	sassafras	-	-	-	1	36	-
Tilia americana	American basswood	1	420	-	1	1	-
Ulmus rubra	slippery elm	7	4400	1/-	3	69	-

[1]Non-native species.

Shrubs were found in most of locations monitored, but no shrubs were found on the microplots on Maryland Heights (Table 35).

Table 35. Shrub density and richness in Harpers Ferry.

Plot	Shrubs	Shrubs / ha	Species
HAFE-30	14	1600	1
HAFE-39	-	-	-
HAFE-61	-	-	-
HAFE-74	-	-	-
HAFE-118	2	240	1
HAFE-154	46	5400	1
HAFE-215	21	2500	2
Total	83	1400	3

Only two shrub species were found in the park. There were 65 spicebush (*Lindera benzoin*) shrubs and 66 seedlings, and 18 American bladdernut (*Staphylea trifolia*) shrubs and nine seedlings.

Forest Pests and Diseases

Gypsy moth was found on a single blackgum (*Nyssa sylvatica*) tree on HAFE-61 on Maryland Heights.

Exotic Plant Species

Exotic Trees

The only exotic trees found on the plots were four trees and one seedling of tree of heaven (*Ailanthus altissima*) and one tree of sweet cheery (*Prunus avium* [Table 34]).

Vines on Trees

All but one plot had vines growing on trees (Table 36).

Table 36. Presence of vines in Harpers Ferry.

Plot	Trees	Trees with Vines	Trees with Vines in Crown
HAFE-30	18	6	2
HAFE-39	28	2	-
HAFE-61	30	8	5
HAFE-74	24	-	-
HAFE-118	16	5	3
HAFE-154	19	3	1
HAFE-215	21	8	3
Total	146	32	14

Only one exotic vine present was found growing on trees in the plots (Table 37). A Japanese honeysuckle was found on plot HAFE-30, in West Virginia east of Bakerton Rd.

Table 37. Species of vines in trees in Harpers Ferry.

Latin Name	Common Name	Trees with Vines	Tree with vines in crown
[1]*Lonicera japonica*	Japanese honeysuckle	1	-
Parthenocissus quinquefolia	Virginia creeper	12	5
Toxicodendron radicans	poison ivy	10	6
Vitis spp.	wild grape	13	7

[1] Non-native species.

Exotic Herbaceous Plants

Exotic herbaceous species were found on all plots in Harpers Ferry (Table 38).While exotics were found throughout the park, on five of the plots they were on less than half the quadrats.

Table 38. Presence of exotic herbaceous plants in Harpers Ferry.

Plot	Quadrats with Exotics	Number of Exotic Species
HAFE-30	8	4
HAFE-39	2	1
HAFE-61	3	2
HAFE-74	3	2
HAFE-118	12	1
HAFE-154	5	3
HAFE-215	3	2
Total	36	5

Only five species of exotic herbaceous species were found in the park (Table 39). None of these species had a high percent cover where they were detected.

Table 39. Cover of exotic plants in Harpers Ferry.

Latin name	Common name	Plots	Mean % cover on quadrats where present	Mean % cover on all quadrats
Alliaria petiolata	garlic mustard	4	1%	<1%
Duchesnea indica	Indian strawberry	3	2%	<1%
Lonicera japonica	Japanese honeysuckle	3	1%	<1%
Rosa multiflora	multiflora rose	1	2%	<1%
Rubus phoenicolasius	wineberry	4	4%	<1%

Manassas National Battlefield Park

Six forest vegetation plots were monitored in Manassas in 2006 (Figure 8).

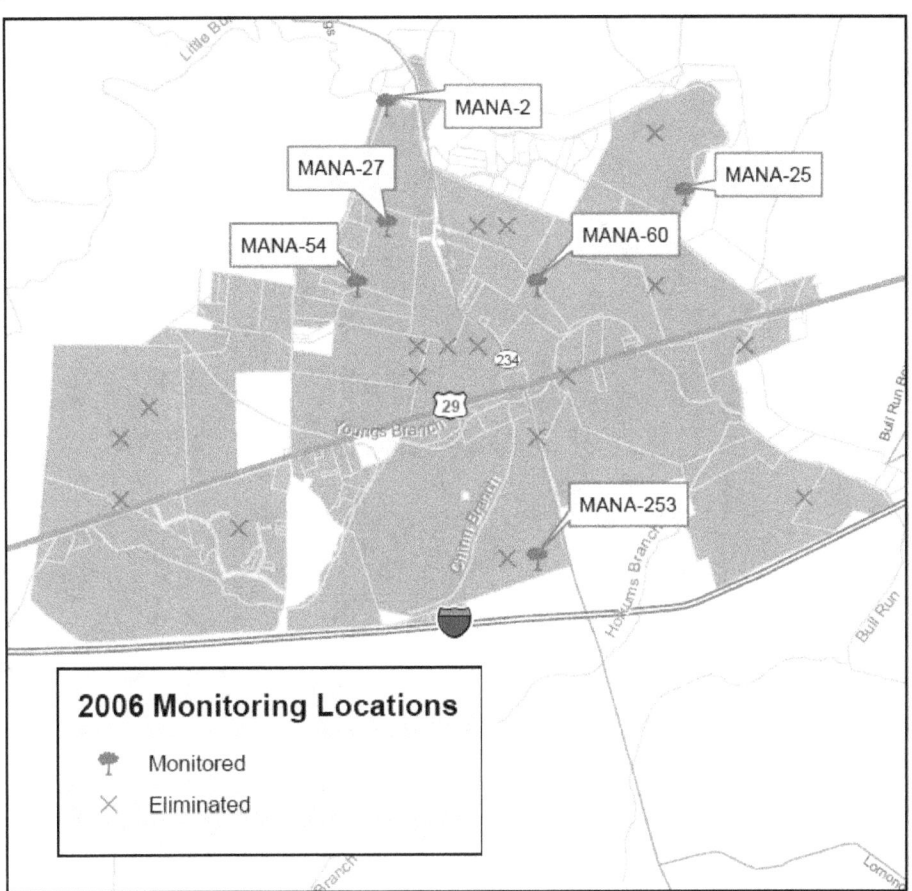

Figure 8. Locations considered for forest monitoring in Manassas.

Forest Communities

There is a high tree density on many of the plots in Manassas (Table 40) but basal area per hectare is not particularly high. All plots have saplings and seedlings on them, unlike many other locations in the NCRN. Twenty seven tree species were found on the plots (Table 41). Tree regeneration was not dominated by any particular species.

Table 40. Density, basal area (BA) and richness of trees, saplings and seedlings in Manassas.

Plot	Trees	Trees/ha	Tree BA cm²	BA/ha	Tree Species	Saplings	Saplings/ha	Sapling BA cm²	BA/ha	Sapling Species	Seedlings	Seedlings/ha	Species
MANA-2	50	710	20,000	290,000	8	6	720	160	19,000	3	20	17,000	3
MANA-25	27	380	18,000	250,000	5	2	240	85	10,000	1	6	5000	4
MANA-27	34	480	14,000	200,000	9	12	1400	210	25,000	7	37	31,000	8
MANA-54	55	780	22,000	310,000	10	10	1200	280	33,000	3	8	6,700	2
MANA-60	25	350	11,000	160,000	7	18	2100	160	19,000	5	14	12,000	3
MANA-253	15	210	8800	120,000	5	10	2300	120	14,000	5	7	5800	3
Total	206	490	94,000	220,000	20	58	1100	100	20,000	14	92	13,000	12

56

Table 41. Tree species found on forest monitoring plots in Manassas.

Latin Name	Common Name	Trees	Tree BA cm^2	Trees with vines/in canopy	Saplings	Sapling BA cm^2	Seedlings
Acer negundo	box elder	17	6400	-	2	85	1
Acer rubrum	red maple	6	2200	-	2	45	-
Asimina triloba	pawpaw	-	-	-	-	-	1
Carya alba	mockernut hickory	17	5100	-	4	50	3
Carya cordiformis	bitternut hickory	7	2400	-	-	-	-
Carya glabra	pignut hickory	10	5800	-	1	2	4
Cercis canadensis	eastern redbud	1	79	-	-	-	2
Cornus florida	flowering dogwood	-	-	-	8	150	-
Diospyros virginiana	common persimmon	-	-	-	1	9	-
Fraxinus pennsylvanica	green ash	11	3300	-	3	87	44
Juglans nigra	black walnut	4	3900	-	-	-	-
Juniperus virginiana	eastern redcedar	66	14,000	1/-	7	260	-
Pinus taeda	loblolly pine	1	290	-	-	-	-
Pinus virginiana	Virginia pine	6	3300	-	-	-	-
Platanus occidentalis	American sycamore	1	2400	-	-	-	-
Prunus serotina	black cherry	-	-	-	3	25	2
Quercus alba	white oak	19	14,000	-	4	15	21
Quercus coccinea	scarlet oak	3	3600	-	-	-	-
Quercus palustris	pin oak	3	3500	-	-	-	-
Quercus phellos	willow oak	1	5300	-	-	-	-
Quercus rubra	northern red oak	12	4900	-	2	40	4
Quercus stellata	post oak	9	8000	-	6	110	-
Sassafras albidum	sassafras	1	140	-	-	-	-
Ulmus americana	American elm	-	-	-	-	-	2
Ulmus rubra	slippery elm	17	7100	-	6	110	1
Viburnum prunifolium	blackhaw	1	84	-	9	30	7

No shrubs were found on the microplots in Manassas, but a total of eight shrub seedlings were encountered (Table 42).

Table 42. Shrub density and richness in Manassas.

Plot	Shrubs	Shrubs/ ha	Species	Seedlings	Seedlings/ha	Species
MANA-2	-	-	-	-	-	-
MANA-25	-	-	-	5	4200	1
MANA-27	-	-	-	-	-	-
MANA-54	-	-	-	-	-	-
MANA-60	-	-	-	2	1700	1
MANA-253	-	-	-	1	830	1
Total	-	-	-	8	1100	3

The seedlings were from three species (Table 43).

Table 43. Shrub species found of forest monitoring plots in Manassas.

Latin Name	Common Name	Shrubs	Shrub Basal Area cm	Seedlings
[1]Elaeagnus umbellata	autumn olive	-	-	2
Lindera benzoin	northern spicebush	-	-	5
Vaccinium stamineum	deerberry	-	-	1

[1]Non-native species.

Forest Pest and Diseases
None of the targeted forest pest or diseases were encountered in Manassas.

Exotic Plant Species
Exotic Trees
No exotic trees were found on the forest monitoring plots.

Vines on Trees
Only a single tree, an eastern redcedar (*Juniperus virginiana*) had a greenbriar vine (*Smilax* sp.) growing on it, which did not reach the crown of the tree.

Exotic Shrubs
Two seedlings from the non-native autumn olive (*Elaeagnus umbellata*) were found (Table 43) on MANA-60.

Exotic Herbaceous Plants

Exotics were found in the quadrats of only four of the six plots in Manassas (Table 44).

Table 44. Frequency of exotic herbaceous plants in Manassas

Park	Quadrats with exotics	Number of exotic species
MANA-2	4	1
MANA-25	11	2
MANA-27	2	2
MANA-54	-	-
MANA-60	6	3
MANA-253	-	-
Total	23	5

None of the five herbaceous exotic species found has a high percent cover (Table 45).

Table 45. Cover of herbaceous exotic plants in Manassas.

Latin name	Common name	Plots	Mean % cover on quadrats where present	Mean % cover on all quadrats
Glechoma hederacea	ground ivy	1	8%	3%
Lonicera japonica	Japanese honeysuckle	2	4%	1%
Microstegium vimineum	Japanese stiltgrass	3	3%	1%
Rosa multiflora	multiflora rose	1	1%	1%
Rubus phoenicolasius	wineberry	1	1%	1%

Monocacy National Battlefield

One forest plot was monitored in Monocacy in 2006 (Figure 9).

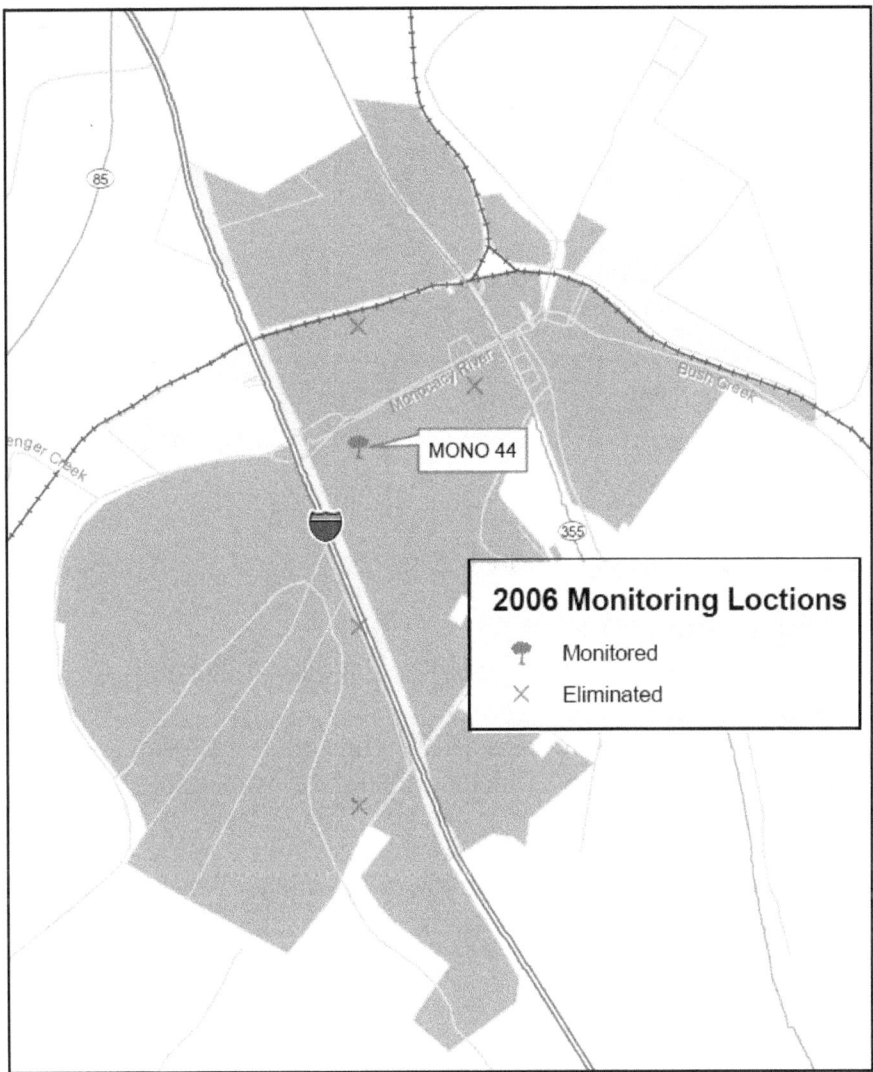

Figure 9. Locations considered for forest monitoring in Monocacy.

Forest Communities

Density and basal area information for the single Monocacy plot can be found in the tables above. In total, six tree species were found on the plot (Table 46).

Table 46. Tree species found on the forest monitoring plot in Monocacy.

Latin Name	Common Name	Trees	Tree BA cm^2	Trees with vines/in canopy	Saplings	Sapling BA cm^2	Seedlings
Acer negundo	box elder	16	2500	3/2	3	150	2
Acer saccharinum	silver maple	13	8100	1/1	1	50	-
[1]*Ailanthus altissima*	tree of heaven	1	810	1/-	-	-	-
Celtis occidentalis	common hackberry	-	-	-	-	-	14
Prunus serotina	black cherry	1	760	1/-	-	-	-
Robinia pseudoacacia	black locust	7	2400	-	-	-	-

[1]Non-native species.

No shrubs were found on the Monocacy plot.

Forest Pests and Diseases
No targeted forest pests or diseases were found on the Monocacy plot.

Exotic Plant Species
One exotic tree was found on the plot, a tree of heaven (*Ailanthus altissima* [Table 46.]).

Six individual trees had vines growing on them. Two trees had Virginia creeper (*Parthenocissus quinquefolia*) and four trees had wild grape (*Vitis* sp.) which reached the crown on three of them. No exotic vines were found.

All 12 quadrats in the Monocacy plot had exotic herbaceous species. In all, 3 exotic herbaceous species were found (Table 47). Indian strawberry (*Duchesnea indica*) had a high percent cover in the plot.

Table 47. Cover of herbaceous exotic plants in Monocacy.

Latin name	Common name	Plots	Mean % cover on quadrats where present	Mean % cover on all quadrats
Alliaria petiolata	garlic mustard	1	3%	3%
Duchesnea indica	Indian strawberry	1	17%	16%
Microstegium vimineum	Japanese stiltgrass	1	14%	4%

National Capital Parks East

Ten plots were monitored in NACE in 2006 (Figure 10). These included three plots in Piscataway, two plots in Anacostia and Greenbelt, and one plot each in the Baltimore-Washington Parkway, Fort Dupont, and Fort Washington.

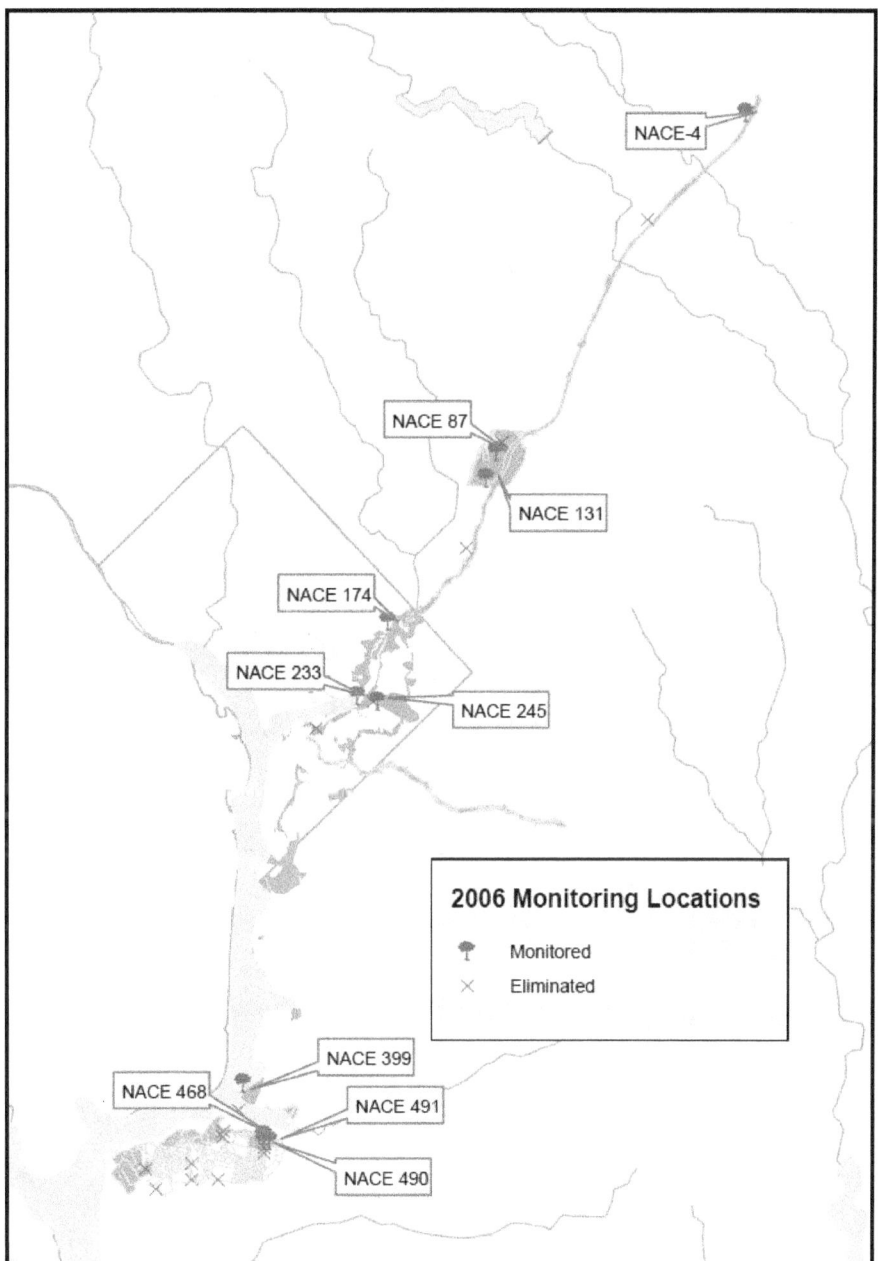

Figure 10. Locations considered for monitoring in National Capital Parks East.

Forest Communities

Tree density and basal area in NACE are not unusual compared to the rest of the region (Table 48).

63

Table 48. Density, basal area (BA) and richness of trees, saplings and seedlings in NACE.

Plot	Trees	Trees/ha	Tree BA cm²	BA/ha	Tree Species	Saplings	Saplings/ha	Sapling BA cm²	BA/ha	Sapling Species	Seedlings	Seedlings/ha	Species
NACE-4	43	610	21,000	290,000	7	6	710	75	8800	5	33	28,000	11
NACE-87	31	440	24,000	350,000	8	6	710	65	7600	1	22	18,000	6
NACE-131	44	620	19,000	270,000	6	1	120	37	4400	1	24	20,000	2
NACE-174	21	300	14,000	200,000	7	7	820	96	11,000	3	29	24,000	6
NACE-233	14	200	13,000	180,000	3	1	120	45	5300	1	-	-	-
NACE-245	12	170	12,000	170,000	7	4	470	78	9200	2	18	15,000	6
NACE-399	20	280	19,000	270,000	8	12	1400	93	11,000	3	12	10,000	2
NACE-468	27	380	17,000	240,000	9	9	1100	120	14,000	5	5	4200	3
NACE-490	-	-	-	-	-	15	2300	27	3200	1	5	4200	3
NACE-491	29	410	25,000	350,000	10	8	940	95	11,000	3	13	11,000	2
Total	241	340	160,000	230,000	25	69	810	730	8600	19	161	13,000	20

64

One plot in Piscataway Park, NACE-490, is an open area which is growing into forest, so there are no trees on the plot, but many saplings. Most plots show some evidence of regeneration, except for plot NACE-233 in Anacostia Park. This plot has only one sapling and no seedlings. Overall, 33 tree species were found on the ten plots in NACE (Table 49).

Table 49. Tree species found on the forest monitoring plots in NACE.

Latin Name	Common Name	Trees	Tree BA cm^2	Trees with vines/in crown	Saplings	Sapling BA cm^2	Seedlings
Acer negundo	box elder	4	2400	4/-	1	7	1
Acer rubrum	red maple	52	20,000	15/3	7	90	12
Acer saccharinum	silver maple	2	1500	2/2	-	-	-
Asimina triloba	pawpaw	-	-	-	16	120	18
Carya cordiformis	bitternut hickory	4	1700	-	-	-	-
Carya glabra	pignut hickory	2	2200	2/1	2	35	-
Cornus florida	flowering dogwood	-	-	-	-	-	1
Diospyros virginiana	common persimmon	2	340	-	15	27	5
Fagus grandifolia	American beech	3	3900	3/-	2	43	1
Fraxinus americana	white ash	2	1300	1/-	2	33	4
Fraxinus pennsylvanica	green ash	4	1000	-	2	14	8
Ilex opaca	American holly	5	800	-	1	37	1
Juniperus virginiana	eastern redcedar	3	1800	2/2	1	18	1
Liquidambar styraciflua	sweetgum	48	24,000	20/7	11	110	57
Liriodendron tulipifera	tulip poplar	21	33,000	12/3	1	26	8
[1]*Malus baccata*	Siberian crabapple	-	-	-	1	17	-
Morus rubra	red mulberry	-	-	-	1	17	-
Nyssa sylvatica	blackgum	28	7300	9/6	1	42	6
Pinus virginiana	Virginia pine	11	9600	-	-	-	1
Platanus occidentalis	American sycamore	4	12,000	4/2	1	1	-
Prunus serotina	black cherry	7	8500	5/-	-	-	14
Quercus alba	white oak	4	5300	3/-	1	30	6
Quercus coccinea	scarlet oak	2	3800	-	-	-	2
Quercus phellos	willow oak	1	2000	1/-	-	-	-
Quercus prinus	chestnut oak	2	270	1/1	-	-	-
Quercus rubra	northern red oak	5	2700	4/1	1	9	1
Quercus stellata	post oak	1	1200	-	-	-	-
Sassafras albidum	sassafras	-	-	-	-	-	13
Tilia americana	American basswood	5	6200	5/1	-	-	-
Ulmus rubra	slippery elm	19	10,000	11/4	1	45	1
Viburnum prunifolium	blackhaw	-	-	-	2	8	-

[1]Non-native species.

The number and basal area of shrubs varied greatly across NACE (Table 50).

Table 50. Shrub density and richness in NACE.

Plot	Shrubs	Shrubs/ha	Species
NACE-4	-	-	-
NACE-87	1	120	1
NACE-131	-	-	-
NACE-174	22	2600	3
NACE-233	30	3500	1
NACE-245	-	-	-
NACE-399	7	820	1
NACE-468	3	350	1
NACE-490	-	-	-
NACE-491	1	120	1
Total	64	760	5

Spicebush (*Lindera benzoin*) is the most common native shrub in NACE (Table 51).

Table 51. Shrub species found on forest monitoring plots in NACE.

Latin Name	Common Name	Shrubs	Seedlings
Ilex verticillata	common winterberry	1	-
Lindera benzoin	northern spicebush	31	39
[1]*Lonicera maackii*	amur honeysuckle	30	-
Vaccinium corymbosum	highbush blueberry	1	-
Viburnum dentatum	southern arrow wood	1	-

[1]Non-native species.

Forest Pests and Diseases
No targeted forest pests or diseases were found in NACE.

Exotic Plant Species
Exotic Trees
The only exotic tree found was a single sapling of Siberian crabapple (*Malus baccata*) on NACE-174 in Anacostia Park.

Vines in Trees
Vines are very common on trees in NACE. Over 43% of all trees have vines in them, and over 13% have vines in their crowns (Table 52). Of these, over 20% of all trees in NACE have exotic vines on them, and nearly 7.5% have exotic vines in their canopy.

Table 52. Presence of vines in NACE.

Plot	Trees	Trees with Vines	Trees with Vines in Crown
NACE-4	43	23	-
NACE-87	31	14	6
NACE-131	44	-	
NACE-174	21	9	-
NACE-233	14	12	4
NACE-245	12	1	-
NACE-399	20	1	1
NACE-468	27	26	15
NACE-490	-	-	-
NACE-491	29	19	7
Total	241	104	33

Table 53. Species of vines in trees in NACE.

Latin Name	Common Name	Trees with Vines	Tree with vines in crown
[1]*Ampelopsis brevipedunculata*	porcelainberry	3	2
[1]*Hedera helix*	English ivy	15	2
[1]*Lonicera spp.* (including *L. japonica*)	honeysuckle	27	12
Parthenocissus quinquefolia	Virginia creeper	24	2
[1]*Rosa multiflora*	multiflora rose	4	2
Smilax spp.	greenbriar	21	7
Toxicodendron radicans	poison ivy	30	10
Vitis spp.	wild grape	21	12

[1]Non-native species

Exotic Shrubs
Japanese honeysuckle (*Lonicera maackii*), an exotic species, has a high number of individuals (Table 51), but is found only on NACE-233 in Anacostia Park.

Exotic Herbaceous Plants
Eight out of ten plots in NACE had exotic species the two exceptions being plot NACE-131 in Greenbelt and NACE-399 in Fort Washington (Table 54).

Table 54. Frequency of exotic herbaceous plants in NACE.

Park	Quadrats with exotics	Number of exotic species
NACE-4	8	3
NACE-87	1	1
NACE-131	-	-
NACE-174	12	4
NACE-233	11	4
NACE-245	6	2
NACE-399	-	-
NACE-468	9	3
NACE-490	1	1
NACE-491	10	5
Total	58	10

Most exotics species had a fairly low percent cover, except for English ivy (*Hedera* helix [Table 55]). English ivy covers much of plots NACE-174 and NACE-233 in Anacostia Park, and is present to a lesser extent on NACE-245 in Fort Dupont Park.

Table 55. Cover of herbaceous exotic plants in NACE.

Latin name	Common name	Plots	Mean % cover on quadrats where present	Mean % cover on all quadrats
Alliaria petiolata	garlic mustard	2	1%	<1%
Ampelopsis brevipedunculata	porcelainberry	1	6%	1%
Clematis terniflora	sweet autumn	1	5%	<1%
Duchesnea indica	Indian strawberry	2	3%	1%
Glechoma hederacea	ground ivy	1	2%	<1%
Hedera helix	English Ivy	3	27%	16%
Lonicera japonica	Japanese honeysuckle	5	4%	2%
Microstegium vimineum	Japanese stiltgrass	4	17%	3%
Polygonum perfoliatum	mile-a-minute	2	4%	1%
Rosa multiflora	multiflora rose	3	2%	<1%

Prince William Forest Park

Thirty-five plots were monitored in Prince William in 2006. The plots were located throughout the park (Figure 11).

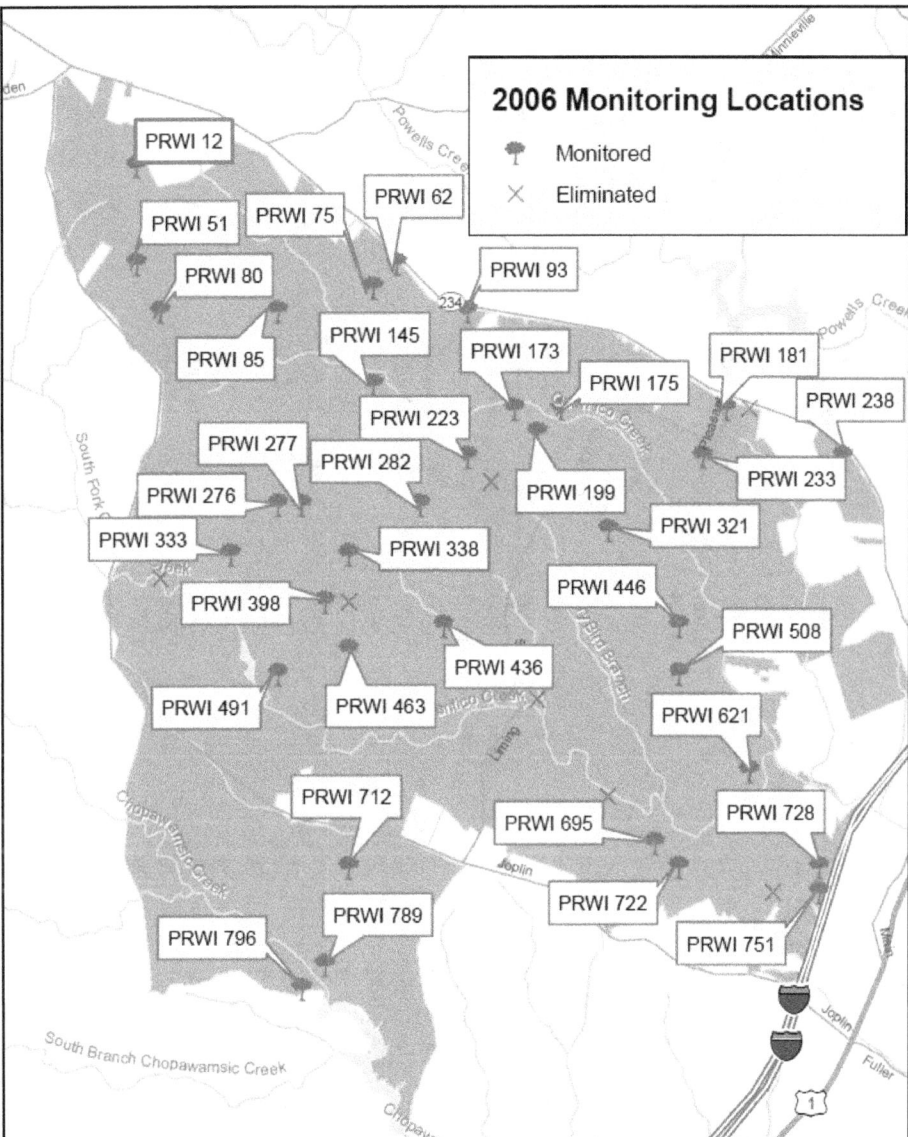

Figure 11. Locations considered for forest monitoring in Prince William.

Forest Communities

Tree and sapling density at Prince William is higher than at most other parks in the region (Table 56). Basal area of trees and density of saplings and seedlings are near the regional mean.

Table 56. Density, basal area (BA) and richness of trees, saplings and seedlings in Prince William.

Plot	Trees	Trees /ha	Tree BA cm²	BA/ha	Tree Species	Saplings	Saplings/ ha	Sapling BA cm²	BA/ha	Sapling Species	Seedlings	Seedlings /ha	Species
PRWI-12	32	450	18,000	250,000	8	7	830	150	18,000	3	7	5800	5
PRWI-15	25	350	20,000	280,000	8	12	1400	140	17,000	6	12	10,000	5
PRWI-62	19	270	20,000	280,000	5	3	350	80	9000	2	2	1700	2
PRWI-75	33	470	21,000	290,000	8	8	940	60	6600	2	5	4200	2
PRWI-80	30	420	14,000	200,000	8	12	1400	340	40,000	9	43	36,000	6
PRWI-85	26	370	26,000	370,000	8	7	830	170	20,000	2	2	1700	1
PRWI-93	28	400	14,000	200,000	10	8	940	230	27,000	4	8	6700	2
PRWI-145	25	350	19,000	280,000	7	6	710	50	6300	2	16	13,000	4
PRWI-173	24	340	15,000	220,000	10	15	1800	230	28,000	5	12	10,000	4
PRWI-175	36	510	17,000	250,000	7	5	590	120	15,000	3	1	830	1
PRWI-181	59	830	31,000	430,000	7	13	1500	240	28,000	4	5	4200	3
PRWI-199	47	660	21,000	300,000	7	13	1500	180	22,000	4	3	2500	2
PRWI-223	23	330	17,000	240,000	11	11	1300	160	18,000	4	5	4200	5
PRWI-233	17	240	14,000	200,000	6	3	350	17	2100	2	3	2500	3
PRWI-238	41	580	22,000	310,000	8	27	3200	400	47,000	6	3	2500	2
PRWI-276	13	180	9000	130,000	6	-	-	-	-	-	17	14,000	5
PRWI-277	27	380	14,000	200,000	8	9	1100	250	29,000	5	14	12,000	6
PRWI-282	48	680	25,000	360,000	7	17	2000	230	27,000	6	17	14,000	8
PRWI-321	26	370	16,000	230,000	6	5	590	69	8100	3	2	1700	2
PRWI-333	25	350	12,000	160,000	9	29	3400	170	21,000	5	53	44,000	7
PRWI-338	39	550	22,000	310,000	9	9	1100	210	24,000	5	9	7500	3
PRWI-398	41	580	20,000	290,000	9	16	1900	280	33,000	5	11	9200	4
PRWI-436	38	540	20,000	290,000	7	9	1100	150	18,000	6	2	1700	2
PRWI-446	29	410	19,000	270,000	8	8	940	180	22,000	3	3	2500	1
PRWI-463	28	400	14,000	200,000	6	7	830	90	10,000	3	3	2500	3
PRWI-491	23	330	9600	140,000	7	16	1900	200	23,000	6	41	34,000	4
PRWI-508	19	270	20,000	290,000	7	6	710	210	24,000	2	8	6700	1
PRWI-621	23	330	17,000	240,000	11	4	470	32	3800	1	-	-	-
PRWI-695	13	180	20,000	280,000	4	10	1200	70	7700	1	4	3300	3
PRWI-712	42	590	21,000	300,000	8	17	2000	300	36,000	5	2	1700	2
PRWI-722	26	370	19,000	270,000	6	6	710	100	12,000	2	4	3300	3
PRWI-728	38	540	21,000	300,000	9	13	1500	370	43,000	7	5	4200	1
PRWI-751	28	400	12,000	170,000	9	7	830	210	25,000	4	12	10,000	4
PRWI-789	40	570	29,000	400,000	10	2	240	62	7300	1	1	830	1
PRWI-796	21	430	15,000	220,000	6	14	1600	250	29,000	3	1	830	1
Total	1052	430	650,000	260,000	27	354	1200	6000	20,000	18	336	8000	22

70

Thirty three different tree species were found in Prince William (Table 57). Virginian pine (*Pinus virginiana*) is the most abundant species as adult trees, but only two seedlings were found, which is likely due to forest succession (US Forest Service 1990).

Table 57. Tree species found on the forest monitoring plots in Prince William.

Latin Name	Common Name	Trees	Tree BA cm^2	Trees with vines/in crown	Saplings	Sapling BA cm^2	Seedlings
Acer rubrum	red maple	76	23,000	2/1	24	470	9
Acer saccharinum	silver maple	4	1400	-	-	-	-
Acer saccharum	sugar maple	1	3000	-	-	-	-
[1]*Ailanthus altissima*	tree of heaven	-	-	-	-	-	3
Amelanchier laevis	Allegheny serviceberry	1	87	-	-	-	4
Asimina triloba	pawpaw	-	-	-	-	-	10
Carpinus caroliniana	American hornbeam	8	750	-	11	110	6
Carya alba	mockernut hickory	48	18,000	1/-	5	150	16
Carya cordiformis	bitternut hickory	3	630	13/1	-	-	-
Carya glabra	pignut hickory	21	16,000	-	2	8	9
Castanea dentata	American chestnut	-	-	-	3	12	4
Cornus florida	flowering dogwood	10	4600	-	21	530	2
Fagus grandifolia	American beech	158	41,000	-	111	1500	28
Fraxinus americana	white ash	3	500	-	-	-	-
Fraxinus pennsylvanica	green ash	1	340	-	-	-	-
Ilex opaca	American holly	20	2700	1/-	50	550	44
Juglans nigra	black walnut	24	27,000	-	-	-	-
Juniperus virginiana	eastern redcedar	6	1500	2/-	5	100	-
Liquidambar styraciflua	sweetgum	6	1200	2/-	1	5	1
Liriodendron tulipifera	tulip poplar	145	130,000	1/-	2	130	3
Nyssa sylvatica	blackgum	89	24,000	6/2	59	1500	7
Pinus taeda	loblolly pine	2	1500	-	-	-	-
Pinus virginiana	Virginia pine	219	160,000	19/1	-	-	2
Prunus serotina	black cherry	4	2900	-/-	-	-	2
Quercus alba	white oak	122	110,000	5/-	37	300	143
Quercus coccinea	scarlet oak	70	73,000	-	2	3	18
Quercus falcata	southern red oak	5	7100	-	4	100	1
Quercus prinus	chestnut oak	7	7100	-	-	-	-
Quercus rubra	northern red oak	16	9000	-	7	180	8
Quercus stellata	post oak	6	7100	-	1	50	-
Quercus velutina	black oak	1	570	-	-	-	-
Sassafras albidum	sassafras	-	-	-	8	270	10
Viburnum prunifolium	blackhaw	-	-	-	-	-	5

[1]Non-native species.

Shrubs were scattered in Prince William (Table 58).

Table 58. Shrub density and richness in Prince William.

Plot	Shrubs	Shrubs per ha	Species
PRWI-12	-	-	-
PRWI-15	-	-	-
PRWI-62	17	2000	1
PRWI-75	3	350	1
PRWI-80	-	-	-
PRWI-85	-	-	-
PRWI-93	1	120	1
PRWI-145	-	-	-
PRWI-173	-	-	-
PRWI-175	-	-	-
PRWI-181	-	-	-
PRWI-199	-	-	-
PRWI-223	15	1800	2
PRWI-233	-	-	-
PRWI-238	-	-	-
PRWI-276	-	-	-
PRWI-277	4	470	1
PRWI-282	2	240	2
PRWI-321	-	-	-
PRWI-333	-	-	-
PRWI-338	6	710	1
PRWI-398	-	-	
PRWI-436	-	-	-
PRWI-446	-	-	-
PRWI-463	3	350	1
PRWI-491	2	240	1
PRWI-508	-	-	-
PRWI-621	-	-	-
PRWI-695	-	-	-
PRWI-712	8	940	2
PRWI-722	-	-	-
PRWI-728	-	-	-
PRWI-751	-	-	-
PRWI-789	-	-	-
PRWI-796	-	-	-

Only two species of shrubs were found in the microplots (Table 59).

Table 59. Shrub species found on the forest monitoring plots in Prince William.

Latin Name	Common Name	Shrubs	Seedlings
Kalmia latifolia	mountain laurel	58	51
Vaccinium corymbosum	highbush blueberry	3	-

Forest Pests and Diseases
No targeted forest pests or diseases were found in Prince William.

Exotic Plant Species
Exotic Trees
The only exotic trees found were three seedlings of tree of heaven (*Ailanthus altissima*) on PRWI-751, which is located in the south east of the park, close to I-95.

Vines on Trees
Relatively few trees have vines growing on them (Table 57). Most of the vines that are growing on trees are *Smilax spp* (Table 60).

Table 60. Species of vines in trees in Prince William.

Latin Name	Common Name	Trees with Vines	Tree with vines in crown
[1]*Lonicera spp.* (including *L. japonica*)	honeysuckle	5	-
Parthenocissus quinquefolia	Virginia creeper	2	1
[1]*Rosa multiflora*	multiflora rose	1	-
Smilax spp.	greenbriar	44	3
Toxicodendron radicans	poison ivy	3	1

[1]Non-native species.

Exotic Shrubs
No exotic shrubs were found on the Prince William plots

Exotic Herbaceous Plants
Few of the plots at Prince William had exotic herbaceous plants present (Table 61). Only three species were found (Table 62) none of which had a high percent cover.

Table 61. Presence of exotic herbaceous plants in Prince William.

Plot	Quadrats with Exotics	Number of Exotic Species
PRWI-12	-	-
PRWI-15	-	-
PRWI-62	-	-
PRWI-75	-	-
PRWI-80	-	-
PRWI-85	-	-
PRWI-93	-	-
PRWI-145	-	-
PRWI-173	1	1
PRWI-175	-	-
PRWI-181	2	2
PRWI-199	-	-
PRWI-223	-	-
PRWI-233	-	-
PRWI-238	3	2
PRWI-276	-	-
PRWI-277	-	-
PRWI-282	-	-
PRWI-321	3	1
PRWI-333	-	-
PRWI-338	1	2
PRWI-398	-	-
PRWI-436	-	-
PRWI-446	-	-
PRWI-463	-	-
PRWI-491	-	-
PRWI-508	-	-
PRWI-621	-	-
PRWI-695	-	-
PRWI-712	-	-
PRWI-722	-	-
PRWI-728	-	-
PRWI-751	4	3
PRWI-789	-	-
PRWI-796	2	1
Total	16	3

Table 62. Cover of herbaceous exotic plants in Prince William.

Latin name	Common name	Plots	Mean % cover on quadrats where present	Mean % cover on all quadrats
Duchesnea indica	Indian strawberry	4	1%	<1%
Lonicera japonica	Japanese honeysuckle	3	1%	<1%
Microstegium vimineum	Japanese stiltgrass	5	4%	<1%

Rock Creek Park

Three forest plots were monitored in Rock Creek in 2006 (Figure 12).

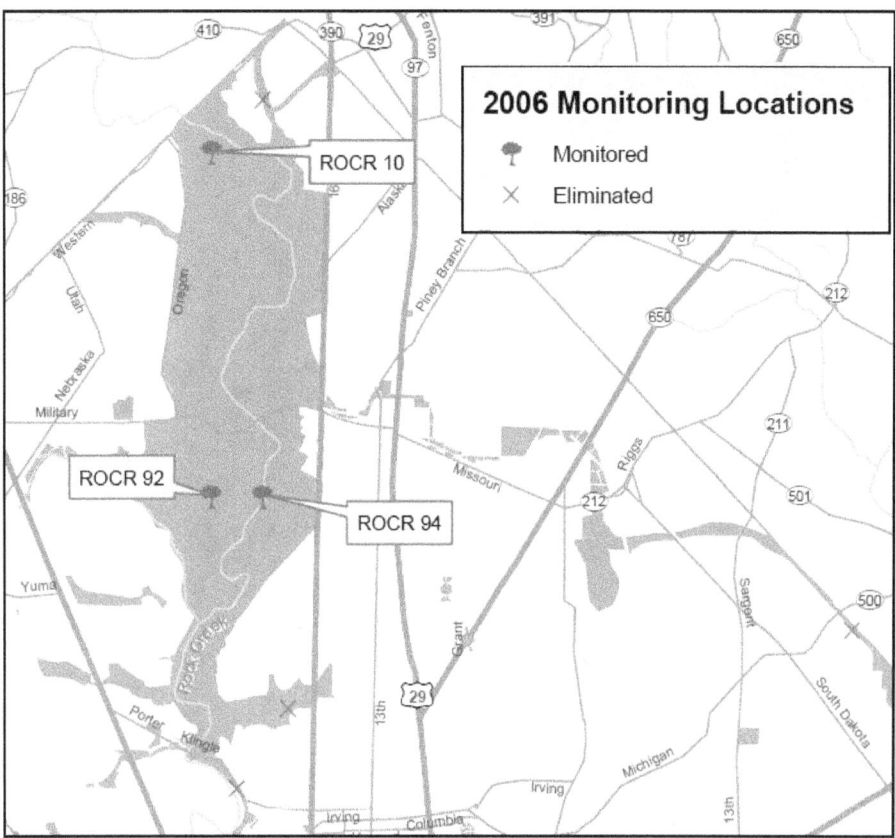

Figure 12. Locations considered for forest monitoring in Rock Creek.

Forest Communities

While tree basal area is above average for the region, sapling density and basal area and seedling density are below average (Table 63). Sixteen tree species were found in Rock Creek (Table 64).

Table 63. Density, basal area (BA) and richness of trees, saplings and seedlings in Rock Creek

Plot	Trees	Trees /ha	Tree BA cm^2	BA/ha	Tree Species	Saplings	Saplings/ ha	Sapling BA cm^2	BA/ha	Sapling Species	Seedlings	Seedlings /ha	Species
ROCR-10	20	280	29,000	410,000	4	8	940	55	6500	1	-	-	-
ROCR-92	9	130	7200	100,000	5	-	-	-	-	-	2	1700	1
ROCR-94	20	280	26,000	360,000	9	11	1300	130	15,000	4	4	3300	3
Total	49	230	62,000	290,000	13	19	750	180	7200	4	6	1700	4

Table 64. Tree species found on the forest monitoring plots in Rock Creek.

Latin Name	Common Name	Trees	Trees with vines/ in crown	Tree BA cm^2	Saplings	Sapling BA cm^2	Seedlings
Acer negundo	box elder	-	-	-	-	-	2
[1]*Acer platanoides*	Norway maple	-	-	-	1	1	-
Acer rubrum	red maple	2	-	290	1	3	-
Amelanchier laevis	Allegheny serviceberry	1	-	93	-	-	-
Carya alba	mockernut hickory	3	-	3300	-	-	-
Cornus florida	flowering dogwood	1	-	110	-	-	-
Fagus grandifolia	American beech	16	3/3	14,000	14	170	-
Fraxinus americana	white ash	1	-	110	3	6	1
Liriodendron tulipifera	tulip poplar	4	-	12,000	-	-	-
Nyssa sylvatica	blackgum	3	-	1100	-	-	1
Prunus serotina	black cherry	-	-	-	-	-	2
Quercus alba	white oak	9	-	24,000	-	-	-
Quercus coccinea	scarlet oak	4	-	1200	-	-	-
Quercus prinus	chestnut oak	3	2/1	3700	-	-	-
Quercus rubra	northern red oak	1	-	1200	-	-	-
Ulmus americana	American elm	1	1/-	1200	-	-	-

[1]Non-native species.

Only one of the monitoring plots had shrubs present (Table 65).

Table 65. Shrub density and richness in Rock Creek.

Plot	Shrubs	Shrubs/ha	Species
ROCR-10	-	-	-
ROCR-92	-	-	-
ROCR-94	2	240	2
Total	2	80	2

Three shrub species were found (Table 66).

Table 66. Shrub species found on forest monitoring plots in Rock Creek.

Latin Name	Common Name	Shrubs	Seedlings
[1]*Euonymus alatus*	winged burning bush	1	2
Kalmia latifolia	mountain laurel	1	-
Viburnum acerifolium	mapleleaf viburnum	-	13

[1]Non-native species.

Forest Pests and Diseases
No targeted forest pests or diseases were found in Rock Creek.

Exotic Plant Species
Exotic Trees
The only exotic tree on the plots was a single sapling of Norway maple (*Acer platanoides*) in plot ROCR-94

Vines in Trees
Few vines were found in trees (Table 64). Of the ten vines found, six are of the exotic species porcelainberry (*Ampelopsis brevipedunculata* [Table 67]).

Table 67. Species of vines in trees in Rock Creek.

Latin Name	Common Name	Trees with Vines	Tree with vines in crown
[1]*Ampelopsis brevipedunculata*	porcelainberry	6	4
Campsis radicans	trumpet creeper	1	-
Smilax spp.	greenbriar	3	2

[1]Non-native species.

Exotic Shrubs
One shrub and two seedlings of winged burning bush (*Euonymus alatus*) were found in plot ROCR-94.

Exotic Herbaceous Plants
Only one of the plots in Rock Creek had exotic herbaceous species (Table 68).

Table 68. Presence of exotic herbaceous plants in Rock Creek.

Plot	Quadrats with Exotics	Number of Exotic Species
ROCR-10	-	-
ROCR-92	12	3
ROCR-94	-	-
Total	12	3

Three exotic herbaceous species were present, of which garlic mustard (Alliaria petiolata) had the highest percent cover (Table 69).

Table 69. Cover of herbaceous exotic plants in Rock Creek.

Latin name	Common name	Plots	Mean % cover on quadrats where present	Mean % cover on all quadrats
Alliaria petiolata	garlic mustard	1	33%	30%
Ampelopsis brevipedunculata	porcelainberry	1	7%	2%
Duchesnea indica	Indian strawberry	1	2%	<1%

Wolf Trap National Park for the Performing Arts

One forest plot was monitored in Wolf Trap in 2006 (Figure 13).

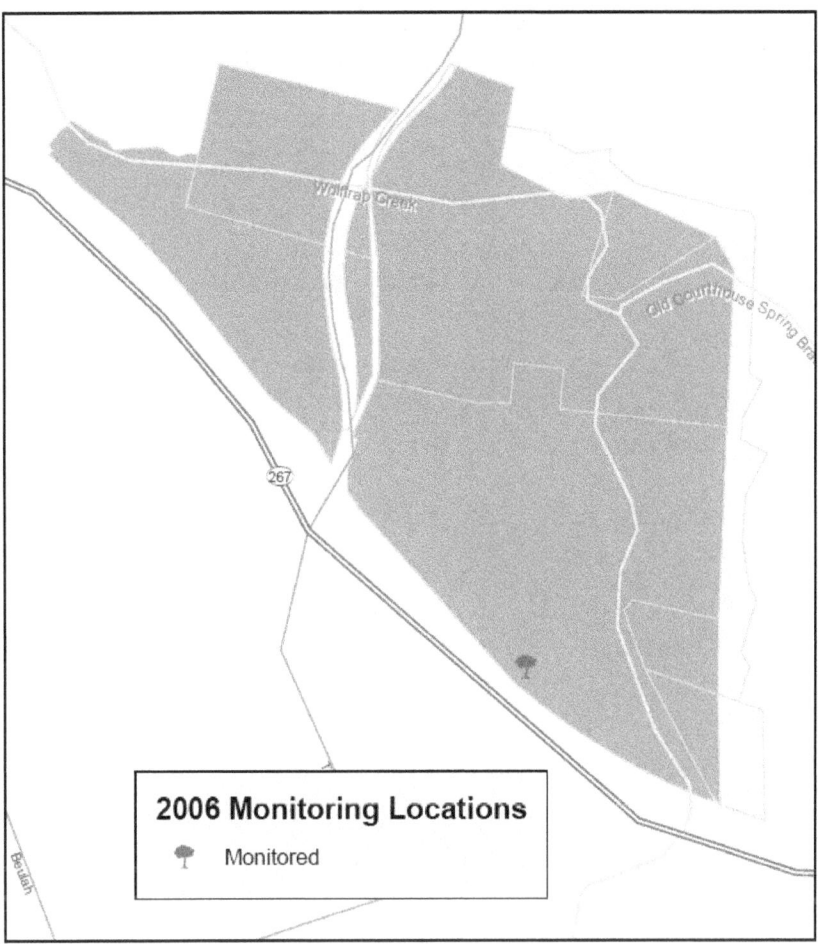

Figure 13. Locations considered for forest monitoring in Wolf Trap.

Forest Communities

Density and basal area information for the single Wolf Trap plot can be found in the tables above. In total, thirteen tree species were found on the plot (Table 70).

Table 70. Tree species found on the forest monitoring plot in Wolf Trap

Latin Name	Common Name	Trees	Tree BA cm^2	Trees with vines/ in crown	Saplings	Sapling BA cm^2	Seedlings
Acer rubrum	red maple	2	290	-	-	-	-
Fagus grandifolia	American beech	1	140	-	-	-	-
Fraxinus americana	white ash	-	-	-	-	-	8
Ilex opaca	American holly	-	-	-	-	-	4
Juniperus virginiana	eastern redcedar	-	-	-	-	-	1
Liriodendron tulipifera	tulip poplar	3	1100	-	-	-	-
Nyssa sylvatica	blackgum	2	230	-	8	220	-
Pinus virginiana	Virginia pine	41	26,000	4/-	-	-	-
Quercus alba	white oak	-	-	-	2	64	-
Quercus prinus	chestnut oak	-	-	-	1	25	-
Quercus rubra	northern red oak	2	250	-	-	-	-
Sassafras albidum	sassafras	2	400	-	-	-	2
Viburnum prunifolium	blackhaw	-	-	-	1	5	-

[1]Non-native species.

No shrubs are found in the microplots of the forest monitoring plot.

Forest Pests and Diseases
No targeted forest pests or diseases were found in Wolf Trap.

Exotic Plant Species
Exotic Trees
No exotic trees were found on the plot in Wolf Trap.

Vines in Trees
Only four trees have vines growing on them on the forest monitoring plot. All four vines are poison ivy (*Toxicodendron radicans*).

Exotic Shrubs
No exotic shrubs were found on the plot in Wolf Trap.

Exotic Herbaceous Plants

Only one exotic herbaceous plant was found, *Microstegium vimineum*, in a single quadrat. It covered 66% of that quadrat for an average of 6% of the plot being covered.

Literature Cited

Dawson, D. 2006. Protocol for Monitoring Forest-Nesting Birds in National Park Service Parks. USGS, Patuxent Wildlife Research Center, Laurel, MD.

National Park Service. 2005. Long-Term Monitoring Plan for Natural Resources in the National Capital Region. Inventory and Monitoring Program, Center for Urban Ecology, Washington DC.

Schmit J.P., Chojnacky, D.C., and Milton, M. 2006. National Capital Region Network Long-Term Forest Monitoring Protocol. National Park Service.

Stevens, D.L. and A. N. Olsen. 2004. Spatially balanced sampling of natural resources. Journal of American Statistical Association. 99(465): 262-278.

Stolte K., Conkling B., Campbell S., and Gillespie A. 2002. Forest Heath Indicators, Forest Inventory and Analysis Program. USDA Forest Service. FS-746.

U.S. Forest Service (USFS). 1990. Silvics of North America. Volume I: Conifers. Agriculture Handbook 654. USFS, Washington D.C.

Van Wagner C.E. 1968. The line intersect method in forest fuel sampling. Forest Science 14: 20-26.

Appendix A

List of forest pests and diseases targeted for monitoring in 2006.

- Beech bark disease
- Butternut canker
- Gypsy moth
- Hemlock wooly adelgid
- Spruce budworm

Appendix B.

Woody plants monitored as shrubs in 2006.

Latin Name	Common Name
Clethra spp.	pepper bushes
Elaeagnus umbellata	autumn olive
Euonymus alatus	winged burning bush
Hamamelis virginiana	American witch hazel
Ilex verticillata	common winterberry
Kalmia latifolia	mountain laurel
Ligustrum obtusifolium	border privet
Lindera benzoin	northern spicebush
Lonicera maackii	amur honeysuckle
Rhus spp.	sumac
Staphylea spp.	bladdernut
Symphoricarpos orbiculatus	coralberry
Vaccinium corymbosum	highbush blueberry
Viburnum acerifolium	mapleleaf viburnum
Viburnum dentatum	southern arrow wood
Viburnum prunifolium	blackhaw

Appendix C.

List of herbaceous exotic plants monitored in 2006.

Latin Name	Common Name
Akebina quinata	five-leaved akebina
Alliaria petiolata	garlic mustard
Ampelopsis brevipedunculata	porcelain berry
Berberis thunbergii	Japanese barberry
Celastrus orbiculatus	oriental bittersweet
Centaurea biebersteinii	spotted knapweed
Cirsium arvense	Canada thistle
Clematis ternifolia	yam-leaf clematis
Duchesnea indica	Indian strawberry
Euonymus fortunei	creeping euonymus
Glechoma hederacea	ground ivy
Hedera helix	English ivy
Hermerocallis fulva	common daylily
Lespedeza cuneata	Chinese lespedeza
Lonicera japonica	Japanese honeysuckle
Lonicera spp.	honeysuckles
Microstegium vimineum	Japanese stiltgrass
Polygonum cuspidatum	Japanese knotweed
Polygonum perfoliatum	mile-a-minute
Pueraria montana	kudzu
Ranunculus ficaria	lesser celandine
Rosa multiflora	multiflora rose
Rubus phoenicolasius	wineberry
Vinca minor	periwinkle

NPS D-71 June 2007